HEAL Your Body, Mind, and Heart

Your Guided Wellness Journal for Self Love, Self Compassion, Healing, and Self Growth

Lana Fayad

Coming Back Home to Yourself

AUTHORITY
PUBLISHING

Second Edition, 2025

Paperback ISBN: 978-1-965480-22-9

eBook ISBN: 978-1-965480-20-5

Published by: Authority Publishing

www.authority-publishing.com

Printed in the United States of America.

Disclaimer

Breathe and Make Time for Yourself.

Empower and Heal Your Body, Mind, and Heart.

This journal belongs to:

"Your life has a purpose. Your dreams count and your voice matters. The meaning of life is to find your gift. Find it in your heart."

I have a dream

Heal (By The Wellness Box)

"Why are you knocking at every other door? Go, knock at the door of your own heart." **- Rumi**

HEAL Your Body, Mind, and Heart

By The Wellness Box

The Wellness box is a unique self-care concept created by Lana Fayad to help you reconnect with your natural state of well-being.

Restore your balance through a daily mindful routine to heal and empower your body and heart.

Learn to manage your stress and release your pain by practicing self-healing techniques and applying writing therapy.

Explore your inner world and empower yourself with the Wellness Journal.

Your journey of self-care and self-love begins now.

You are loved. You are protected.

Contents

Auhor's Note

"Heal" is Coming Back Home to Yourself.

The mind keeps repeating what the heart needs to heal.

"To the heart in you, don't be afraid to feel.

To the sun in you, don't be afraid to shine.

To the love in you, don't be afraid to heal.

To the silence in you, don't be afraid to break."

From the moment we are born until we take our last breath, our life's journey is all about love.

At its core, our journey is about the heart: we spend our lives searching for love and longing for it. When we cannot find it, we struggle, we suffer, and life feels meaningless.

Much of the pain we experience throughout our lifetime stems from a lack of love:

Our childhood insecurities often arise from the absence of love and the rejection we felt from parents, teachers, or friends.

Our troubled relationships result from neglected love and the indifference of one partner toward the needs of the other.

The pain of grief comes from the loss of love we experience after losing our loved ones. We do not simply mourn their absence; we grieve the loss of their love, warmth, connection, and presence that once filled our hearts and lives.

These painful experiences make giving and receiving love the hardest thing to do. With every wound we endure, we instinctively build walls around our hearts to protect ourselves from more suffering. *We are not afraid of love; we only run from old pain.* We close our hearts and move on, pretending that all is well. Yet, deep within, we still carry the weight of our unhealed childhood traumas, emotional scars, personal and ancestral stories, and even the collective pain of an entire nation. In almost every challenge we face, these unresolved wounds resurface, disrupting the flow of our lives, reminding us that we are still stuck and that all we need is to break free and heal.

To heal is to touch with love what we once touched with fear. Whenever you find yourself overwhelmed with anger, sadness, fear, or judgment, remember that this part of you that is hurting the most, at its deepest essence, needs your love the most.

Healing is not about striving for perfection or fixing what's broken—it is about embracing and loving the parts of you that have suffered and nurturing what's been neglected.

Only love has the power to truly heal; love is the language of healing.

When we *allow* ourselves to truly feel, gently open our hearts, and dare to meet our shadows and deeply buried emotions,

When we *accept* our painful stories with love and compassion, recognizing them as integral parts of our journey of growth and evolution,

Only when we *unlearn* what we have been taught and instead choose to carry our *hearts* with pride, free from guilt, shame, or judgment, embracing who we are as we are, can we begin to heal.

> ***The peace, joy, and freedom we seek are on the other side of the pain we don't want to feel. Healing is the process of releasing everything that holds us back from growth and true freedom. We cannot heal if we resist pain or change; our hearts need to soften to let the light in once more.***

It's time to stop running from yourself and start feeling the depth within. You are meant to express what is hurting you, what you need, and who you truly are. Each time you move away from your heart's desires and your soul's calling, you take a step closer to suffering, illness, and pain. Choose to honor your truth and step into alignment with your authentic self.

In this journal, I invite you to find your way home to yourself and deeply explore your true essence, to uncover that sacred place of love where your soul resides. This space, your *heart*, is the gateway to your existence. Open it. Heal it from within. Release the energy of fear and pain, and welcome back the energy of love.

The love you have spent your life searching for has always been within you.

It is **You**. *Love is your true essence.*

Your soul holds the blueprint of your life. It knows the way; trust it to guide you. You are destined for what is written in your heart.

Allow yourself to become who you were always meant to be.

Now is the time to reclaim your power and stand fully in your truth.

Now is the time for rebirth; let it happen.

Because life is, and will always be, about *love*, I dedicate this book to the beautiful journey of healing, transformation, and love.

Lana

Introduction

Why and How to Use This Book

What is "Heal my wellness journal"?

When did you last feel you were a human BEING, not a human DOING?

Don't be afraid of the new love; learn that you are only afraid of the old pain.

Heal is to touch with love, what we used to touch with fear.

Revealing the secrets of healing that everyone should know to navigate their life in a healthier way.

Essential healing techniques, tools, and guidance are gathered in one book to heal your whole being, body, mind, and heart.

You are about to start a beautiful journey of coming back home to yourself, a journey of healing, self-discovery, and empowerment, an exploration of your true essence that has the potential to change your entire life.

The ancient definition of "heal" means "to make whole," and that is the book's purpose: to heal all the parts of you that have been broken, forgotten, or lost over time. It acknowledges the deep connection between your body, mind, and heart and highlights the importance of addressing all three simultaneously. We are not just a body, a mind, or a heart; we are a combination of all three, each affecting the others. This is why it's essential to heal these aspects together.

'Heal' is the ultimate guide to living a healthier life. It is a therapeutic experience offering the opportunity to liberate yourself and embrace your wholeness. By embracing the multifaceted dimensions of your being, you unlock the gateway to your fullest potential.

Returning to your true self, understanding your core needs, and embracing your authenticity are key steps toward lasting health and fulfillment.

This book reminds you of who you are and what you once loved. **It is a roadmap to reconnect with your heart, the home of your soul**. We came to this earth with a purpose, and it is time to remember it.

The book helps you:

- Build a strong self-care routine, develop positive habits, and deepen your relationship with yourself.
- Improve your physical and mental health through mindful practices.
- Release emotional pain with effective stress management techniques, helping you align with your heart's truth.

The root of much of our discomfort, illness, and frustration lies in our detachment from our hearts and disconnection from ourselves. If trauma represents this disconnection, then healing is the process of reconnection.

We often detach from ourselves as a coping mechanism in the face of suffering and fear. Fear governs much of our lives—fear of the unknown, of death, of losing something or someone... Any physical or mental symptom is a signal from our bodies that we are not okay and have strayed from our authentic selves.

Within the pages of this book, you'll embark on an inner journey guided by tools and exercises designed to reconnect you to your natural state of well-being. You'll uncover the patterns that hold you back and release the emotional pain and blockages that hinder your growth.

"It is not what you do but how you do it.

It is not what you see but how you look at it.

It is not how your life is; it is how you live it."

Why use the book?

Three reasons to use this book: the 3R

1. **Reconnecting with your authentic self**
2. **Reduce anxiety and heal your emotional pain**
3. **Rewiring your brain to transform your life**

1- Reconnecting With The Authentic Self

The path to better physical and mental health begins with a profound return to authenticity. We often feel compelled to conform to social expectations, suppressing our true selves and heart desires. Healing is about shedding the layers of inauthenticity that have accumulated over time and rediscovering the core of our being. ***The act of healing is fundamentally about reconnecting with***

ourselves. It's the journey toward wholeness and a return to our true nature.

Embracing Individuality

As we progress towards authenticity, we embrace our individuality and unique needs. This means allowing ourselves to express our emotions, needs, desires, and aspirations without fear of judgment or rejection. Much of our discomfort and disease stems from not being ourselves, not knowing who we are, and not being free to live as we wish. Our discomfort often arises from the compulsive need to play a role that does not align with our true selves. The loss of our authenticity is often an adaptive response to our early environment, where we were forced to suppress our needs and emotions to be accepted by our community.

Self-Acceptance and Self-Love

Reconnecting with the authentic self requires self-acceptance and self-love. It involves acknowledging that every experience, including trauma, has played a significant role in our journey. Healing begins when we start being compassionate and gentle with ourselves.

2- Reduce Anxiety

Reducing anxiety involves a combination of psychological, emotional, and lifestyle strategies.

Here are some techniques you can find in the book to help you foster a deeper connection with the authentic self and alleviate anxiety:

Deep Breathing Exercises

Engage in deep breathing exercises to calm your nervous system and reduce anxiety. Focus on slow, deep breaths to center yourself.

Journaling

Keep a journal to explore your thoughts, emotions, and experiences. Writing can be a powerful tool for self-reflection and understanding your inner world.

Mindfulness and Meditation

Practice mindfulness and meditation to become more aware of your thoughts, emotions, and bodily sensations. This can help you understand your feelings and connect with your inner self.

Gratitude Practice

Cultivate a daily gratitude practice to shift your focus toward positive aspects of life. This can increase feelings of contentment and connection to your heart.

Self-Compassion

Be kind and compassionate toward yourself. Avoid self-criticism and negative self-talk. Treat yourself as you would a good friend.

Mind-Body Practices

Engage in mind-body practices like yoga. These activities can help integrate your mental and physical well-being.

Connect with Loved Ones

Maintain meaningful relationships and social connections. Sharing your thoughts and feelings with loved ones can provide emotional support.

Set Healthy Boundaries

Establish clear boundaries to protect your emotional well-being. Learning to say "no" when necessary can reduce stress and anxiety.

Practice Self-Care

Prioritize self-care activities that nourish your soul and bring you joy to your heart.

Positive Affirmations

Use positive affirmations to challenge negative thought patterns and foster a more positive self-image.

Remember that everyone's journey to connect with their authentic self and reduce anxiety is unique. It may take time and experience to find the strategies and techniques that work best for you. A holistic approach that combines several of these methods can be especially effective in promoting emotional well-being and inner connection.

3- Rewiring Your Brain Through Journaling

Your brain is constantly changing; this is called "neuroplasticity." Even though your brain is a physical structure, it changes based on what you think, feel, choose, eat, and more. As you think, feel, and make decisions, you generate quantum energy waves through your brain, and your brain responds electromagnetically and chemically.

We have the ability to direct the plasticity process in our favor and restructure our brains.

Brain building takes *work* and requires a long-term commitment. It takes 21 days to break down your thoughts and start the building process, but real neuroplasticity happens after 63 days. If you want to change your old patterns and recreate the future, the journal Heal is here to help you achieve this goal. Inside the journal, there is a 12-week program (63 days) for rewiring your brain and changing your overall routine, habits, and thoughts.

The Importance of Journaling

Journaling uses both the left and right sides of the brain, which means you can simultaneously process your thoughts and feelings.

Journaling is a highly effective tool for stress relief; it reduces stress by serving as an emotional release of negative thoughts and feelings and helps with problem-solving and keeping things in perspective. When you're writing down your thoughts and feelings, you're able to manage your anxiety and exteriorize them instead of repressing them in your body, down to the level of your cells, which might lead with time to physical or mental illness.

Journaling about your feelings is **linked to decreased mental distress**. In a study, researchers found that those with various medical conditions and anxiety who wrote for 15 minutes three days a week over 12 weeks had increased feelings of well-being and fewer depressive symptoms after one month.

Using journaling as a tool for well-being encourages you to get to know yourself better, be more present in the moment, and develop a greater awareness of your emotions and thought patterns. It also helps you create a healthy routine throughout the year, month by month, and day by day.

How to Use The Book

The book unfolds in 3 parts.

PART I - My Life and Wellness Goals (Mind)

This part of the book is designed to help you reflect on yourself and gain more insight and awareness of the things you love. The aim is to mindfully integrate more of what makes you happy into your routine, set goals that align with who you truly are, and make plans to cultivate habits that will help you become a better and happier version of yourself.

In this section, you'll begin by welcoming yourself fully, embracing all three aspects—body, mind, and heart—with a primary focus on the mind. The 63-day program is designed to help rewire your brain, supporting you in changing habits and creating positive transformation.

PART II - My Wellness Manual (Body and Mind)

In this section, you delve into practical application. You'll learn various wellness and healing tools and techniques, including deep breathing, mindfulness, yoga, and meditation, to care for your body and mind and calm your nervous system.

Part III - My Healing Space (Heart)

This section is dedicated to managing your mental health and emotional well-being. It serves as your private sanctuary to release negative emotions, unwind, and de-stress whenever needed. Here, your heart takes center stage. You'll learn to recognize your value, embrace both pain and joy, and find that natural love is always inside you. This section is a place for forgiving, healing, and loving yourself.

What Results to Expect After Using the Book

Through this journey of self-discovery and transformation, you will learn how to:

- RECLAIM your personal ***POWER*** over your health and life so that you can reach your goals faster and more easily.
- Meet your ***true self*** again and reconnect to your heart and soul's purpose.
- DESIGN an ideal SELF-CARE and ***self-healing routine*** to help you positively navigate your life.
- Learn ***stress management techniques***, including breathing exercises, yoga, mindfulness, and meditation.
- Release your emotional pain and ***deal effectively with anxiety.***
- BOOST your emotional health, self-confidence, and self-esteem.
- Address your physical, mental, and emotional needs.
- Rediscover ***self-love.***
- Unlock the secrets of ***energy healing***.
- BUILD a strong relationship with yourself to tap into your true POTENTIAL.

Make time for yourself with "Heal," our wellness journal, and **start each day with a fresh mind.**

When life gets busy, it can be difficult to prioritize your well-being. Pausing for a few moments in the morning or evening can help you get back in touch with what's really important. You can use the pages of the wellness journal to reflect on what makes you feel good—setting goals, tracking healthy habits, and noting down what you're grateful for. With a little practice, your wellness journal will become a treasured tool to turn to whenever you need a feel-good boost.

To complement your reading experience, we invite you to explore the workbook version of this book. Download the ebook at www.healbythewellnessbox.com/heal-workbook and access unlimited templates to support your healing journey. Use it to track your progress and deepen your self-reflection for years to come.

Heal

1. Self-awareness heals
2. Talking about our pain heals
3. Motion heals
4. Yoga and Meditation heal
5. Breathing and Mindfulness techniques heal
6. Music and Sound heal
7. Journaling heals
8. Food heals
9. Helping others heals
10. Nature heals
11. Love heals

How to Start?

Every day, dedicate 10 minutes or more to focusing on this journal. It will help you create your new wellness routine and reset your mind to embrace this new belief:

Self-care is a priority.

Then, start scheduling your time to focus on healthy self-love activities to implement in your life.

Take a serious look at how much you give to others versus how much you give to yourself. Pause for a moment and see where you fall:

On average, how much of your time do you put towards self-care versus caring for others?

- 25% Self—75% Others
- 40% Self—60% Others
- 50% Self—50% Others
- 60% Self—40% Others
- 75% Self—25% Others

Now You Can Tell Where You Stand.

Until we take the time to stop, rest, and refuel, we compromise our health and lower our capacity to help those we love.

**"You cannot pour from an empty cup,
take care of yourself first."**

- Start thinking of your pre-scheduled "me time" as sacred.
- Release any feelings of guilt and schedule a time (20 to 60 min) each day to focus on yourself and no one else, whether early morning or evening: you can go for a walk or run, do yoga, etc.
- Admit you can always find a way to engage in some self-nurturing activity.

And Always Remember:

**"You deserve the love you freely give to
others."**

Self-Care Tips

Detach – Escape – Nurture – Heal

The following list of self-care tips includes activities that givers and busy people should intentionally incorporate into their routines. This will help them balance their needs with those of others.

1- Detach

- Take some time off —take a break from your giving activities as you would take time off from work;
- Say "NO!"—learn to set boundaries and let go of toxic situations, negative people, and unnecessary guilt.
- Spend time with people you love: friends, family, and your partner.

2- Escape: Reclaim Yourself

- Take a walk in nature — Reconnect and re-engage physically with nature.
- Treat yourself to something special, and remind yourself of what you deserve: a time to feel special and acknowledge your worth and value.
- Engage in arts and creative endeavors: you might discover new and in-

teresting ways to relax.

3- Nurture: Restore, Replenish

- Eat well and improve your nutritional intake—good health, stamina, and energy levels are directly affected by what we eat.
- Physical Activity: Regular exercise directly impacts your physical and mental health.
- Sleep well and get proper rest—it is during deep and restful sleep that the body heals and replenishes; we run the risk of physical and mental fatigue and compromise our immune systems when we don't sleep well.

4- Heal: Ground Yourself and De-Stress

- Breathing, yoga, and meditation are great ways to de-stress, heal, and calm both body and mind.
- Center yourself: Take some time to reconnect with your goals and purpose in life, engage in self-reflection, and do soul-searching.
- Freehand writing in a journal—journal writing is a way to release thoughts and emotions that build up over time; it's also a great way to formulate goals and track your self-care progress.

Welcome to Heal, the Wellness Journal

"Wellness is a state of complete physical, mental, and social well-being, and not merely the absence of disease or infirmity." – The World Health Organization

It is the active process of becoming aware of and making choices toward a healthy and fulfilling life.

Well-being is a state of being healthy and happy.

This book is your ultimate guide to wellness, self-love, and self-healing.

It will help you develop the ability to practice self-care and stress management techniques.

Learn how to maintain a healthy body and mind with our wellness journal.

"Heal" is a profound experience waiting to unfold. Let the magic of transformation and healing begin.

PART I - My Life and Wellness Goals

This is your personal tool to set your self-care goals, track them on a monthly and weekly basis, develop your new overall wellness routine and transform your mental patterns in just 63 days.

PART II - My Wellness Manual

Reconnect to your natural state of well-being by practicing different types of wellness and healing techniques: breathing, mindfulness, yoga, and meditation.

PART III – My Healing Space

This part is designed to help you manage your mental health and emotional well-being. It is your private space to release any negative emotions, unplug and de-stress each time you need to escape.

We Heal By Unfolding Our Truth One Layer at a Time.

Why is healing important? It allows us to reclaim our power, put the pieces back together, and emerge stronger than before. Healing sets us FREE.

How do we heal? By changing the old, negative version of ourselves and unlearning the old patterns and paradigms of thinking that stop us from living our lives fully. When we first acknowledge the origin of it, we learn to accept it, heal it, and move on from it so we can be free.

Learn how to take charge of your own life and health by first liberating your emotional blockages. Listen to your body and your heart to detect the root cause of your physical or emotional pain.

What techniques can we use to heal? There are many healing techniques; the most effective ones are the techniques that can help you heal your heart and release the root cause of your emotional, mental, and physical pain. Biodecoding[1] and ancestral healing are two of those techniques.

You can check www.healbythewellnessbox.com

For more information about our healing techniques/programs or book a call with us, visit www.healbythewellnessbox.com/book-call.

This book can guide you through various self-healing techniques to alleviate stress or emotional pain (refer to parts 2 and 3).

---

1. Biodecoding®: is a pioneering technique to decode any kind of symptom (physical and emotional) and resolve its underlying bio-emotional cause through a signature methodology. It is a complementary approach to any conventional and alternative treatments and has the potential to unlock and speed up the healing process.

Part I - My Life, My Wellness Goals

This is your personal tool and roadmap to setting your self-care goals (step 1), tracking them monthly (step 2) and weekly (step 3), and developing your new overall wellness routine.

My Life

Reconnect With Yourself.

This part of the book is designed to help you reflect on yourself and gain more insight and awareness of the things you love.

The aim is to mindfully integrate more of what makes you happy into your routine, set goals that align with who you truly are, and make plans to cultivate habits that will help you become a better and happier version of yourself.

"If you can't figure out your purpose, figure out your passion. For your passion will lead you right into your purpose."

One Life, Just One

Why do we hold ourselves back from living the life we love?

What is holding us back from living it?

Fear? What fear?

We are all born with LOVE.

FEAR is something we learn.

Unlearn the fear, reload love, and dare to live.

50 Questions to Change Your Life and Remember Who You Are

We get so busy in our daily lives that we drift away from ourselves, our hearts, feelings, dreams, and the things and people we love. These questions remind you of your true self and put you back on the right track. Let us start fresh, prepare ourselves to return to the essence, and begin from here.

Take your time answering these questions. Some may be difficult to answer, but that's okay. Do not judge yourself; find your answer through the energy of love, compassion, and acceptance. Remember, we have all gone through tough times, experienced failures, and faced challenges. We came to earth to learn our lessons and keep ourselves connected to the source, heart, and soul.

50 Questions to Change Your Life and Remember Who You Are

I- Meeting Myself

1.□Who are you? How would you describe yourself?

____

____

____

2.□What makes you happy? What makes you feel alive?

____

____

____

3.□What is your heart's deepest desire?

____

____

____

4.□What did you use to love the most when you were a little child? What did you use to enjoy doing?

____

____

____

5. What is the one thing (or more) you can't live without, and if it is missing, life has no more meaning to you? (music, nature, love, values...)

____

____

____

"We are all trying to heal from the hidden
and forgotten wounds."

6.□Who are you without fear, guilt, shame, or judgment? Who are you at the very core of your being?

____

____

____

7.□What does your heart need the most right now (safety, love, joy...)? Are you listening to your heart?

____

____

____

What can you do to give your heart what it needs? Maybe to take action, maybe to ask for help or support, to make the change that you need, to stop, take a break and breathe for a moment, to be grateful, to be gentle with yourself, to be less judgmental or less worrying or less overthinking.)

II- My Dreams

Your dreams are special notes from your soul.

8. What is your passion? If you don't know your passion, remember when you were completely aligned with your heart.

____

____

____

9.□What are your dreams in life?

____

____

____

10. What's stopping you from living the life of your dreams?

Try to find the answer within you; don't blame others; remember we have always the choice to be and do what we want.

____

____

____

"When it comes down to it, there are two ways to approach our lives: either as the victims or the creators of our lives."

11. What baby steps can you take to get closer to your dreams?

____

____

____

12. What is your heart whispering to you every day?

____

____

____

13. If the 'little you' looks at you right now, what advice will they give you? A message or a reminder.

____

____

____

III- My life now

14.□Look at your life now. Are you happy? Are you doing what makes you happy? What is missing?

Check again your answers to question 2. What changes do you need to make in your life to start creating your happiness? What is stopping you from making those changes? Remember, there is always a way.

____

____

____

15.□During the past 24 hours, how much time did you spend caring for yourself?

____

____

____

"Don't lose the music of your heart."

16.□What does it mean to you to be alive? While you are living every day, how much are you alive? How can you be more alive?

17.□What are the top priorities in your life right now? Are you on your list?

18.□What gives your life a real meaning?

19.□Is there something you're still holding on to, and is it time to let it go?

"It is not true that people stop pursuing dreams because they grow old, they grow old because they stop pursuing dreams."

20.□Are you putting any parts of your life on hold? Why?

Remember that the fear of change is normal. Allow yourself to step out of your comfort zone. We have always the choice to evolve or stay the same.

____

____

____

21.□What are you busy with today? Will this matter one year from now? Three years? 5 years?

____

____

____

22.□What would you do if you had one year to live?

____

____

____

23.□What advice would you give yourself three years ago?

____

____

____

24.□What advice will your future self give you now?

____

____

____

25.□What would your biggest regret be if you were to die tomorrow? What can you do now to stop this regret from happening?

____

____

____

"I am healing, learning, and growing every single day. It is a gradual process that I have full faith in."

IV- My inner-self

26. What is your inner dialogue like? Critical, destructive, judgmental... or compassionate and loving?

___

___

___

27. What bad habits/patterns do you want to break?
Overthinking, giving others more importance and value than yourself, living in fear and guilt all the time...

___

___

___

28. What good habits do you want to cultivate?
Respecting and accepting yourself, enjoying being alive, taking care of your body, mind, and heart...

___

___

___

29. What are your inner strengths? And your weaknesses?
Remember to love them both.

___

___

___

30. Do you spend time regretting the past, resisting changes, or allowing yourself to learn and accept to move on? Do you practice acceptance, or are you playing the victim and always blaming others?

31. Do you spend your time focusing on your blessings or on what you are missing?

Notice if you are only focusing on what you lack. You will attract more of this energy. Learn to focus on what you have. Maybe you are just busy comparing your life with others. Remember, we are not born to be perfect; we are born to be real.

32. Do you love yourself? Why or why not? What is stopping you from loving yourself?

33. How can you love yourself more today?

34. What are you proud of about yourself? What are your biggest achievements?

35. What are the hidden parts of you that require healing? Are you willing to heal and be free?

36. What would you do if you knew you could not fail? If there were no judgment, no fear, how would you live?

"These mountains that you are carrying,
you were only supposed to climb."

V- The Meaning of My Life

37. Where are you living now, past, future, or present? Are you living in acceptance or resistance to life?

____

____

____

38. What is your purpose in life? Why do you exist? What is your soul mission? Remember, you came to earth for a reason, mostly to learn and evolve. If you don't know yet the purpose, search for your passion.

____

____

____

39. What are your talents/gifts?

____

____

____

"I know there are days when you feel like giving up, but I think it is brave that you never do."

40. How can you make your life more meaningful, starting today?

41. What drives you? When are you most inspired, most motivated, and most charged up? How can you do more of that starting today?

42. When are you most stressed? How can you do less of that?

43. What are the two things you need to get rid of so you can enjoy life more? (Overthinking, judging, worrying, comparing, controlling...)

"Life is a dance between your deepest desire and your greatest fear."

VI- My People

44. Who is/are your life's most important person(s) now?

____

____

____

45. Are you giving them enough time and real attention? How can you spend more time with them starting today?

____

____

____

46. Are you afraid of letting others get close to you? Why?

____

____

____

47. Who are the five people you spend the most time with? Are these people lifting you or holding you back?

In both cases, you are responsible for your own choices.

"Talking about our problems is our greatest addiction. Let us break the habit & start talking about our joys and blessings."

VII- My Career

48. Do you love your job? If not, what is your ideal career? What have you always dreamt of doing?

49. How can you start creating your ideal career today?

Remember, it is never too late to pursue your dreams.

50. Are you settling for less than what you are worth? Why? Is there anything that you are running away from, maybe your own success?

"You deserve to heal and be happy. Don't be afraid of the new love and the new hope. Learn that you were only afraid of the old pain."

What Are Two Things You're Going To Do Differently After Answering These 50 Questions?

____

____

Now that you have practiced self-reflection and have examined your needs, your heart's desires, and your life in general, you can start taking the necessary steps to create a happier version of yourself that is aligned with who you truly are.

The secret to happiness is freedom, and the secret to freedom is courage.

It takes courage to jump into the unknown, to want a different life, to face your shadows, to try new things, and to choose 'you.'

Step 1- My Wellness Goals

How can you show up for yourself from now on?

How can you nurture your body, mind, and soul?

Set the goals you need the most in your life now.

Body *(eat healthy, workout, sleep more, practice yoga...)*

____

____

____

Mind *(calm your mind, creative mind, positive mind, less worrying...)*

____

____

____

Heart and Soul: What is your dream in life? *(listen to your inner voice, follow your heart...)*

I am going to learn... *(anything you love and need...)*

Here's what I need most... *(what is missing in your life now?)*

I need to do more of what makes me happy... *(Do more of what you love...)*

I would love to spend time with... *(family, friends...)*

A bad habit I am going to break... *(smoking, judging, overthinking...)*

One thing I need to let go and leave behind...

My Major Decisions to Start With	Start Date

Step 2- My Monthly Wellness Goals

"Just when the caterpillar thought the
world was over, she became a Butterfly."

Now, Make It Clearer.

Start by organizing your wellness and life goals month by month, knowing that a goal can take more than one month or even a year to achieve.

Start with the goals you need the most in your life.

The process will be challenging and will take time to complete.

Learn to embrace your life transformation process with ease and acceptance.

Be Gentle With Yourself. Be Patient.

Want to dive deeper into the exercises in this book? The accompanying workbook is available as an ebook at www.healbythewellnessbox.com/heal-workbook, offering unlimited printable templates to help you integrate these practices into your daily life.

My Monthly Wellness Goals

Month / Year

Date: ______________________________

My Gratitude Note

Before you start focusing on what you need to change and what goal you need to achieve, start noticing what is good in your life now. If you start from a place of gratitude and positive energy, you can easily attract what you want.

Write Down What You're Grateful For

I am grateful for

____

I am grateful for

____

I am grateful for

I am grateful for

I am grateful for

My Monthly Wellness Goals

Month / Year

____

Choose the activities you need to focus on this month and add them to your monthly wellness routine.

BODY		
1. Physical activities	2. Eat healthy *(eat the rainbow)*	3. Drink more water / Detox drinks
4. Practice Yoga/breathwork	5. Time in nature	6. Sleep better *(7-8 hours)*

My Steps: When/How?

____

____

____

MIND		
1. Calm the mind/ Meditation	2. Positive mind	3. Journaling / Talk about my stress
4. Digital detox	5. Say no / set boundaries	6. Ask for mental health help

My Steps: When/How?

HEART		
1. Do / Learn something I love	2. Be gentle with myself and others	3. Spend time with people I love
4. Release my emotional pain	5. Be grateful	6. Open my heart to receive and give love

My Steps: When/How?

My Monthly Reflections

"Trust the magic of new beginnings."

The Wellness Tracker

Month / Year

At the end of each month, rate your practice on a scale of 1 to 5.

Did I take care of my body? *(workout, physical activity, enough sleep)*

Did I eat and drink healthily?

Did I do one thing that made me happy?

Did I spend time with people I love?

Did I take care of my mental health and emotional well-being? *(positive self-talk, self-acceptance,...)*

The Wellness Tracker

Month / Year

____

How Am I Feeling?

____

____

If I am not feeling good, what do I need to do to feel better?

(check where applicable and/or add more actions as they apply to you)

_____ Love Myself More

_____ Believe in Myself

_____ Be Patient

_____ More Focused

_____ Be Grateful

_____ Less Negative

What shall I work on next month to improve my wellness performance and get closer to my goals?

____

____

____

Step 3- My Weekly/Daily Wellness Routine

This Section is Your Guide to Creating

A Healthy Weekly/Daily Routine

That will Impact Your Health and Overall Well-Being.

Your Daily Routine Influences

The Quality of Your Life

Make The Right Choices For a Healthier Lifestyle;

The Choices You Make Today will Determine Your Future.

The Five Elements of Life

1- Air

Activity: *Breathe.*

- *I become aware of my breath. I take a mental break from my busy life.*

Tips:

- I sit comfortably and gently close my eyes.
- I bring my awareness to my breath and body: if I am rounding my back, I adjust my posture, sit tall, roll my shoulders slightly backward, and open my chest.
- I place my hands on my belly, close my mouth, and take a nice deep breath in from my nose and a deep breath out from my mouth. I feel the flow of my breath.
- I notice the sensation of my belly expanding with every inhalation and deflating with every exhalation.
- I relax my body and mind.
- I breathe and let go of any tension or pain.
- I do it for ten rounds.

"One day or day one is your decision."

2- Water

Activity: *Stay hydrated.*

Tips:

- I start my day with a cup of warm water and lime.
- I drink 6 to 8 cups of water per day.
- I reduce my intake of coffee and sodas.

3- Earth

Activity: *Eat more from the soil.*

Tips:

- I eat a balanced diet.
- I eat a wide variety of colorful vegetables and fruit: eat the rainbow.
- I eat more food coming from soil that has been exposed to the sun: besides vegetables and fruit, I eat whole grains, lean protein such as beans and lentils, good fats such as olive oil and avocado, seeds such as flax and chia, and nuts.
- I reduce fried, junk, and processed food.
- I avoid dairy products and sugar.

"Be grateful for life, not everyone made it so far."

4- Fire

Activity: *Build energy and heat in my body to burn up impurities and toxins by doing physical activities.*

Tips:

- I go for a walk, to the gym, or practice yoga for at least 30 minutes (try to walk around in nature).
- I park farther away from my destination (work, house...) and take a short walk.
- I take the stairs instead of the elevator.

5- Space

Activity: Create space in my heart.

Tips:

- I choose to live through the open space in my heart.
- I perform random acts of kindness, offer love to those I care about, and smile often, even for strangers.
- I spend one hour of my day fully present and engaged with someone I care about or something I love to do. I do my digital detox: I stay away from my phone.
- I am gentle with myself and others; I don't judge myself or others.

- I am patient and compassionate.

The Healing Power of Nutrient-Rich Foods

Eating a balanced, wholesome diet not only contributes to our physical health but also plays a significant role in improving our overall well-being and emotional state. Certain foods have the power to soothe symptoms and give your body a boost when you have specific illnesses or injuries. Help yourself integrate more of these healing foods into your life.

Superfoods for Optimal Health

Packed with essential nutrients, superfoods act as catalysts for good health and well-being. Their benefits extend beyond the physical aspect, promoting mental health as well. These remarkable foods strengthen our immune systems and contain compounds that reduce inflammation—a key contributor to various diseases. Additionally, some superfoods possess antimicrobial properties capable of fighting harmful bacteria.

The primary goal of incorporating superfoods into our diet is to combat the inflammation caused by stress and the consumption of highly acidic and processed foods. Doing so can shift our body's pH balance towards a more alkaline state, making it less susceptible to diseases. Some notable superfoods in this regard include leafy greens, turmeric, saffron, ginger, oregano (thyme), green tea, nuts and seeds such as cumin, chia, and black seeds, avocado, olive oil, garlic, tomatoes, broccoli, and foods rich in polyphenols, such as dark chocolate and berries, as well as many types of plants and herbs such as moringa, spirulina, and more.

The Connection between Diet and Mental Health

The relationship between our dietary choices and our mental health is multifaceted. Emerging research suggests a strong link between the foods we consume and our emotional well-being. Making thoughtful adjustments to your diet can significantly impact how you feel daily. Here are some practical tips to consider:

1. ***Stay Hydrated:*** Even mild dehydration can affect mood, energy, and concentration. Drink an adequate amount of water throughout the day to stay well-hydrated.

2. ***Balanced Fats:*** Your brain relies on healthy fats to function optimally. Include sources of healthy fats in your diet, such as olive oil, nuts, seeds, oily fish, avocados, and eggs. Avoid trans fats found in processed or packaged foods, as they can negatively affect your mood and heart health.

3. ***Whole Foods from Sun-Exposed Soil:*** Choose foods that are closer to their natural state and grown in nutrient-rich soil with fewer chemicals and preservatives. Incorporate whole grains, fruits, and vegetables into your diet to ensure you receive the essential vitamins and minerals that promote brain and overall health.

4. ***Protein for Mood Regulation:*** Each meal should include some form of protein, as it contains amino acids that your brain uses to help regulate your mood.

5. ***Gut Health Matters:*** Gut health can be a reflection of your emotional state and be influenced by stress. Maintain a healthy gut by consuming fruits, vegetables, beans, and probiotics, which can support your digestive system and overall well-being.

6. ***Caffeine Awareness:*** Be mindful of how caffeine consumption can impact your mood. Excessive caffeine intake, especially close to bedtime,

can lead to sleep problems and increase irritability and anxiety. Caffeine can be found in coffee, tea, cola, energy drinks, and chocolate.

By embracing nutrient-rich superfoods and making thoughtful choices in our diet, we have the power to help our bodies find their natural balance and uplift our mental and emotional well-being. The path to a healthier, happier life begins with the food we choose to fuel our bodies daily.

My Healing Mantras

I Choose Love.

"Negativity brings down your immune system."

What Do You Spend Most of Your Time Thinking About?

Do you know that every cell in your body is affected by the status of your mind?

Stress directly affects our body's biochemistry by increasing inflammation and reducing our ability to repair the damage.

Heal yourself by shifting into a positive mindset.

The word mantra loosely translates to "instrument of the mind." Mantras have the power to transform your thinking and rewire thought patterns and belief systems that have been ingrained deep within your subconscious mind.

Mantras are repeated sounds, words, or phrases that create a desired effect, such as healing or self-awareness.

Challenge unhealthy thoughts by assuming the best in yourself and others.

We all have skills, but we spend our time focusing on our flaws and weaknesses.

You Have The Power to Choose. Choose Happiness and Love.

How to Use These Mantras?

Anytime you experience a negative, destructive, or stressful thought, consciously replace it with the opposite thought and focus on the desired outcome.

Choose a phrase or affirmation that resonates with you and calms or uplifts you. It could be something simple but deeply impactful. Focus on the words that speak most to your heart.

Feel the mantra's energy as you visualize its meaning. Repeat it aloud a few times with your eyes closed, or write it down to anchor its power. Keep repeating it throughout the day, consciously infusing its meaning into your actions whenever possible.

Remember, patience is key. You can't master this overnight—just like building muscle, you must practice, work at it, and cultivate it daily.

For example, during difficult times or when working through painful emotions, try mantras like "This too shall pass" or "I am protected, I am safe." Let the words guide you through the challenge.

My Healing Mantras

You can create your own mantra tailored to what you need most in your life at this moment. Focus on using the present tense and affirm positive statements, avoiding negation. Your mantra should resonate deeply with your heart and spirit. Choose words that uplift and empower you, guiding you toward the balance, peace, or strength you seek.

Let it reflect your true desires, remind you of your inner power, and be a constant source of grounding and inspiration.

1. I am in charge of how I feel today, and I am choosing joy and contentment.
2. I know I am loved and supported as I move through my life.
3. I choose to feel good about myself every day.
4. I am exactly where I need to be.
5. I release my past and forgive myself.
6. Everything I need to heal is already within me.
7. I am protected. I am safe.
8. I use Love to make all the decisions in my life.
9. I move forward with confidence and ease.
10. I trust the process of life: I surrender to the flow of life.
11. I have the power to choose. I choose love and joy.
12. I am gentle with myself.
13. I take charge of my mind and life now.
14. I am willing to heal. Now, I create a safe and new future.
15. I am powerful: I trust life, and I trust myself.
16. I love and appreciate myself. I am enough.
17. I am at peace with myself.

18. I am not perfect, but I love it.

19. I live in the present moment joyously and free.

20. I choose peace; I breathe freely and fully.

21. I let go of unnecessary guilt.

22. I allow the love in my heart to heal me.

23. I am willing to feel. It is safe for me to express my feelings.

24. I am free.

25. I release what no longer serves me.

"When you truly live from the loving space of your heart, everything in your life will flow with ease and harmony."

Studies demonstrated that individuals who repress their negative emotions also suppress their body's immunity, making them more vulnerable to a variety of illnesses.

When You Cultivate Healthy Emotions, You Promote Self-Healing and Self-Regulation in Your Body

What do you need to remind yourself today?

- I am kind.
- I am grateful
- I am strong.
- I am grounded.
- I am loved.
- I am beautiful.
- I am Worthy.
- I am confident.
- I am calm.
- I am peaceful.
- I am protected.
- I am healthy
- I am free
- I am enough
- I am blessed

Instructions for My Daily Routine: A 63-Day Program to Rewire Your Brain

To implement the 63-day program, you can download the workbook at www.healbythewellnessbox.com/heal-workbook. It includes printable templates designed to support your daily practice and help you integrate these transformative exercises into your routine.

"Stress is caused by being 'here' but wanting to be 'there'."

Be present

1. Daily journaling/gratitude.

2. Breathe consciously/breathwork *(refer to "My Breathing Space" in part II of this book).*

3. Eat the rainbow: veggies and fruits. *(refer to the section above on "Earth").*

4. Drink water *(and healthy drinks).*

5. Exercise *(physical activity).*

6. Sleep well.

7. Take care of your heart *(refer to the section above on "Space").*

Based on your monthly goals (body, mind, and heart) and based on the five elements of life, you can start incorporating a new wellness routine into your daily life to rewire your brain in 63 days.

Make sure to commit to at least three healthy daily activities in addition to the daily gratitude note.

Remember, daily choices can impact your health and whole well-being.

If you want to make the change, you must do it for 63 days.

In the accompanying workbook, you will find a 13-week/63-day program to rewire your brain and create a healthier and happier you.

Download your complimentary copy from https://healbythewellnessbox.com/heal-workbook

My Weekly/Daily Wellness Routine

Week / Month / Year

____

Daily Routine	Mon	Tue	Wed	Thu	Fri	Sat	Sun
Gratitude							
Breathe consciously							
Eat the rainbow							
Drink water							
Exercise							
Sleep well							
Heart							

How will I take care of my body, mind, and heart this week?

(make sure to be aligned with your monthly goals)

Body

____

Mind

____

Heart

____

My Daily Check-in and Gratitude Note

When you take the time to focus on the good things in your life, you naturally become more positive.

Expressing gratitude improves mental, physical, and relational well-being.

Gratitude disconnects us from toxic and negative emotions.

Studies have found that giving thanks and counting blessings can help people sleep better, lower their stress levels, and improve their interpersonal relationships.

A Reminder Of What You Can Be Grateful For

- Grateful for my body (to move, breathe, walk, sleep...)
- Grateful for my family, my friends...
- Grateful for my five senses (to be able to see, hear, smell, taste, and touch)
- Grateful for the food, the house, and the work I have
- Grateful for my kind heart (to love, feel, forgive...)
- Grateful for nature (the sun, water, air, trees, animals...)
- Grateful for my mind (intelligent, creative, analytical...)
- Grateful for being unique (no one is me)
- Grateful for my faith, my hope in life...
- Grateful for my kids, for being a mother or a dad...
- Grateful for the little things in my life
- Grateful for the great moments and experiences I had (beautiful trips and vacations, graduation, beautiful lifetime events, and the birth of my kids...)

My Daily Check-in and Gratitude Note

My Daily Check-in and Gratitude Note

Date: Day / Month / Year

Daytime: *Learn to cultivate an authentic connection with yourself. Start each day with mindful awareness, taking a moment to observe your needs and feelings with openness, honesty and care. Acknowledge your internal state without judgment or resistance. Suppressing or denying your feelings and needs can lead to frustration, intensify anger, and perpetuate heavy emotions. Instead, approach yourself with love, compassion, and acceptance. This practice helps you build a healthy relationship with yourself and break free from old, unhealthy patterns.*

Once you've acknowledged your internal state—whether it's joyful or not—shift your focus to the bright aspects of your life by practicing gratitude. A simple note of gratitude has the power to transform even the heaviest emotions, bringing a sense of lightness, clarity, and hope.

Take a deep breath, check in with your heart, and create space to honor and embrace your authentic self.

1- What do you need the most today? How can you respond to your needs?

1 Some Rest	2 Healthy Food/Drink	3 See People You Love	4 Some Fresh Air to Breathe *(Time in Nature)*
5 Say No and Set Boundaries	6 Physical Activity	7 Talk About Your Emotions	8 Fun Activities *(Do More of What You Love)*
9 Sleep Well	10 Some Time Alone	11 Some Love	12 Be Less Negative and More Grateful

2- How am I feeling emotionally? If I'm not feeling well, can I identify the emotion I might be suppressing—anger, sadness, fear, or something else?

What is this emotion trying to tell me about my needs? For example, if you're feeling anxious, it could indicate a need for security.

____

3- Remember My Gifts, Blessings, and Strengths/Positive Self-Talk:

I am ______________________________

I am blessed	I am enough	My feelings are important
I am unique	I am generous	I matter
I am valuable	I am free	I learn to let go
I am safe	I am loved	I welcome love in my life
I am healthy	I am kind	I deserve love and respect
I am a gentle loving human being	I am beautiful (inside out)	I see the good that's already in my life
I am strong	I am protected	I can ask for help if I need it
		It is ok to say no

4- Write Down 3 Things, People, or Situations That You're Grateful For:

I am grateful for:

1. ______________________________

2. ______________________________

3. ______________________________

Night Time: *Write down something that went well or brought you joy during the day.*

1. ______________________________

2. ______________________________

Night Time: *Write down 2 beautiful things you need to do tomorrow to bring joy to your heart. (Remember, you can find joy in simple things: what would your inner child choose to do?)*

1. ______________________________

2. ______________________________

Part II - My Wellness Manual

My Breathing Space

I breathe, I am alive, I am relaxed.

"Every breath is an opportunity to receive and let go: Receive love and let go of pain."

When Was The Last Time You Listened to The Sound of Your Breathing?

Breath is life.

It is the life force that keeps us alive. Yet, breathing is the biological process to which we pay the least attention.

How we breathe influences every area of our lives, including physical and mental health, emotional balance, and overall well-being.

Our breath serves as a barometer of our inner state: when we feel calm, our breathing is smooth and steady; when we are tense, our breath becomes shallow and constricted. Just as our emotions and thoughts influence our breathing patterns, the way we breathe can, in turn, influence and affect our emotions and mental state. This is the profound power of our breath.

"Reconnect to your inner world."

The Power of Our Breath

Mindful, intentional breathing is a powerful tool that energizes our bodies and brings clarity and calmness to our minds. When we allow our breath to flow deeply and fully, we initiate a positive and transformative chain reaction throughout our entire system.

How to Breathe?

Deep breathing sends a signal to our brain that we are safe, which in turn helps our mind and body relax. Remarkably, up to 70% of our body's waste is expelled through our lungs just by breathing naturally. Yet, many of us have never learned how to breathe properly.

By practicing deep breathing, we can break the cycle of stress hormones like adrenaline and cortisol, which are key contributors to anxiety and panic attacks. Breathing fully from the belly engages the parasympathetic nervous system, which slows the heart rate and lowers blood pressure, promoting a state of calm and balance.

The basis for all deep breathing practices originates in the science of yoga, specifically the fourth limb of yoga, known as pranayama. The word pranayama is derived from two Sanskrit words. Although there are various definitions of the term, one interpretation is *prana* (life force) and *Ayama* (expansion), or expanding the life force using the breath. The ancient yogis learned that by controlling the breath, you can influence every aspect of your life.

Medically speaking, "Studies have found that breathing practices can help reduce symptoms associated with anxiety, insomnia, post-traumatic stress disorder, depression, and attention-deficit disorder."

"If you don't pick a day to relax, your
body will pick it for you."

How Do You Breathe? Do You Breathe Correctly?

Exercise 1: Observe Your Breath

Use this exercise to focus on your breath. All you need to do is observe your natural state. It is about being mindful of every breath you put into your body.

- ***Sit comfortably and breathe normally.*** Observe your breath without judgment. Don't try to change it. Is it shallow, short, tight, deep, long, and calm? In all cases, it reflects how you feel at this moment.
- ***Are you breathing from your chest or your belly?*** Short breaths come out of your chest, while deep breaths come from your abdomen. Most people take short, shallow breaths into their chests, which can make them feel anxious and drain their energy.

"Breathe in, slowly, gently, deeply."

In exercise 2, you'll learn how to take deeper breaths all the way into your belly.

Practice the following techniques to learn how to breathe naturally and correctly.

Exercise 2: Learn How to Breathe (Belly Breathing)

- ***Bring your awareness to your body and your posture.*** Sit comfortably and gently close your eyes. If you are rounding your back, adjust your posture, roll your shoulders slightly backward, and open your chest. Your shoulders are relaxed.

(When you develop a healthy posture, the breath is better able to flow into areas of the body that are open and free of tension).

Place your right hand on your belly and your left hand on your chest. Take a deep breath in through your nose and exhale slowly through your mouth. As you inhale, pay attention to the sensation of your belly expanding, feeling it rise under your right hand. Pause for a moment at the top of the breath. Then, as you exhale, feel your belly gently contract, sinking back down. Notice how your right hand moves with each breath while your left hand remains mostly still. Your belly should be doing the work, rising and falling, while your chest experiences only slight lifts.

We are learning to breathe deeply from the abdomen, which is a way to breathe correctly.

Repeat this exercise for ten rounds.

"Deep breaths are like love notes to your body."

Exercise 3: Breathing Techniques for Stress Relief

Your breath is a powerful tool for reducing stress and alleviating anxiety. Incorporating simple breathing exercises into your daily routine can make a significant difference in how you feel. Along with the belly breathing exercise previously described, you can try one of the following techniques:

4-4 Breathing Technique

In this exercise, you'll match how long you breathe in with how long you breathe out.

Sit comfortably on the floor or a chair and close your eyes.

1. Breathe in through your nose to a mental count of four (1 - 2 - 3 - 4).
2. Breathe out through your nose to the same count of four.
3. Repeat at least ten times.

4-7-8 Breathing Technique

Sit comfortably on the floor or a chair and close your eyes. Exhale completely through the mouth.

1. Inhale deeply through the nose for a count of 4.
2. Hold your breath for a count of 7.
3. Exhale completely and release your breath for a count of 8.

4. Repeat several times.

“The quality of your breath expresses your inner feelings.”

Exercise 4: Cleansing Breathing

1. Sit comfortably on the floor or in a chair. Allow your breath to flow naturally through your body. Begin by taking a few deep breaths in and out.

2. Turn your attention inward and connect with your body. If you feel any pain or tension in a particular area, focus on that spot. As you inhale, direct your breath to this place and breathe deeply. Imagine the oxygen flowing to the area, soothing and dissolving the pain or tension as you exhale.

3. Inhale deeply, feeling the breath, bringing your body peace, healing, and nourishment.

4. Exhale fully, releasing any negative emotions or discomfort.

5. Now, introduce a phrase to your breath. As you inhale, silently say, “I breathe in peace and calm.” As you exhale, say, “I breathe out pain and tension.” You can also choose any emotion you wish to release, such as anger or fear, and repeat this phrase with each exhalation: “I let go of any anger or fear, releasing it completely from my body."

6. Continue this practice for a few minutes, allowing the breath to bring you deeper into a state of relaxation and inner calm.

Exercise 5: The Box Breathing or The Four Square Breathing

Sit comfortably, keep the spine straight, and keep your shoulders relaxed.

Close your eyes, take a few breaths in and out, and start the following breathing cycle:

1. Inhale through your nose for 4 seconds (or 3 seconds).
2. Hold your breath inside while counting to 4 (or 3).
3. Exhale slowly through your mouth for 4 seconds (or 3 seconds).
4. Hold your lungs empty for 4 seconds (or 3 seconds).

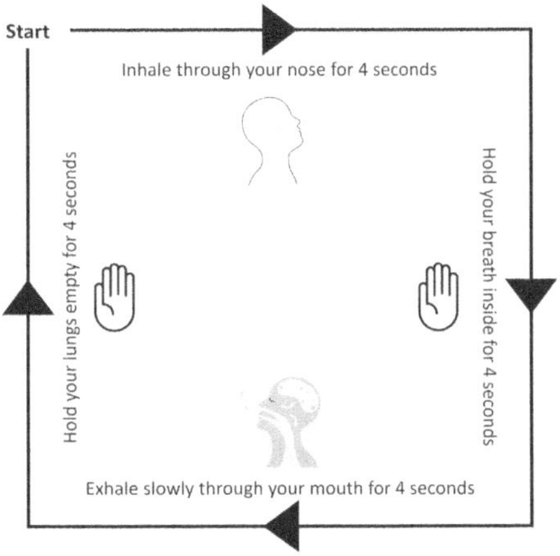

Box Breathing Exercise

Exercise 6: The Alternate Nostril Breathing

In the yogic tradition, practice Alternate Nostril Breathing, known as *Nadi Shodhana*, when feeling anxious or ungrounded. This will immediately help you feel calmer.

- Sit in a comfortable position with your legs crossed.
- Place your left hand on your left knee.
- Lift your right hand toward your nose: close your 2nd and 3rd finger (check the image below)
- Exhale completely, and then use your right thumb to close your right nostril.
- Inhale through your left nostril and then close the left nostril with your fourth finger.
- Open the right nostril and exhale through this side.
- Inhale through the right nostril and then close this nostril.
- Open the left nostril and exhale through the left side.
- This is one cycle. Repeat for up to 2 minutes.
- Always complete the practice by finishing with an exhale on the left side.

Your breathing should be effortless, with your mind gently observing the inflow and outflow of breath.

Stop the exercise and return to your normal breathing if you feel discomfort.

The Alternate Nostril Breathing

Exercise 7: The Heart-Focused Breathing

Whenever you feel overwhelmed or unsettled, try this calming exercise:

- Rub your hands together briskly, creating warmth through the friction.
- Close your eyes and place your warm hands over your heart, feeling the comforting touch.
- Take three deep breaths from your belly, and with each exhale, allow your body to soften and release any tension.
- Tune into your heartbeat, noticing the calmness and softness of your breath under your hands.
- Focus your awareness on your heart center. Visualize a sphere of golden-white light radiating in your chest like a sun, clearing away any anxiety, fear, or sadness. Surrender to the natural flow of your breath and the sense of grounding and safety it brings. Let go completely.
- Visualize your heart center expanding, breath by breath, allowing your breath to flow freely and gently opening and releasing any tightness in your chest.
- Continue this breath of calm and compassion for a few minutes, staying connected to your breathing and heart center.
- Observe any changes in your body and emotions. When you're ready, gently open your eyes.

My Mindful Life

I am present.

"The best way to capture moments is to pay attention. This is how we cultivate mind-fulness."

Are you aware of your body, your feelings, and your thoughts?

Or do you only focus on the external world, get angry about yesterday's events, and worry about tomorrow's?

Do you ever notice that the only real moment is the present moment?

Your life is now.

What is Mindfulness?

Mindfulness is being aware of or bringing attention to this moment, deliberately and without judging the experience. Just be in the moment, in the here and now.

Observe what is happening around you and how it affects you without judgment.

The emphasis is always on "what" is happening, not "why" it is happening. There is no right or wrong experience. Whatever your experience is, this is your experience at this moment.

"Walk as if you are kissing the earth with
your feet."

Why Mindfulness?

Mindfulness seeks to make you aware of your thoughts and emotions so that you can see how they manifest in your body. It helps you be better prepared to respond appropriately and remain calm in challenging situations.

How to Practice Mindfulness?

You can practice mindfulness in several ways during your everyday life.

- You can use breathing exercises or practice yoga (check the chapters on breathing and yoga);
- You can practice meditation or learn to relax your mind by letting go of negative and stressful thoughts.
- Being more aware of your senses can also help you remain more mindful: actively look, listen, smell, feel, or taste. Paying more attention to sensory information makes you more aware of your surroundings.

"Your mind is your instrument. Learn to
be its master and not its slave."

Mindfulness Techniques

Break Negative Patterns by Creating New Positive Pathways

One of the main techniques in mindfulness is to focus on your thoughts and emotions. It helps you switch to more positive mindsets. You become what you think about all day long. The more attention you give to something positive, the better you will feel.

So next time you find yourself trapped in your analytical mind or negative thoughts, remember this:

- I notice my negative and stressed-out mind.
- I slow down momentarily and breathe to bring myself back to the present.
- I accept my thoughts for what they are. There is no need to judge them or to take them too seriously. I let go of them.
- I switch my negative mindset to a positive one by using positive affirmations.

> "Watch your thoughts, notice how you talk to yourself. If it is destructive, judgmental, and negative, stop immediately and recognize this, then say to yourself, OKAY I noticed that and I will change it."

Positive Affirmations

Learn How to Talk to Yourself

Affirmations are great tools for interrupting old or negative thought patterns. An affirmation is a positive, believable thought you choose to immerse your consciousness in to produce the desired result.

Positive self-talk can form new neural pathways in your brain, strengthening the truths that serve you and reducing your attention to what stresses you out.

You control your mind; don't let it control you.

"Allow any negative thoughts to pass you
by like a cloud in the sky."

Positive Awareness/Self-Talk

- I am patient and gentle with myself; I am doing my best right now.
- I allow myself to rest for a moment and relax: I don't need to be doing something at every moment.
- The past is no longer here. It's over. It was real then, but now it's only a part of my imagination.
- I embrace and experience life rather than constantly analyzing it.
- Rather than obsessing over what could be better, I am happy with what is.
- I find my happiness by living in the moment: I take responsibility for my happiness and choose to concentrate on what I have instead of what I

lack.

- I deserve to be happy.
- I deserve love and respect.

If your mind doesn't slow down, try observing and identifying your emotions without having to resolve them. Acknowledge and express your feelings.

(check the last part of the Journal, "My healing space").

"It all begins and ends in your mind. What
you give power to, has power over you.
Your thoughts become your reality."

Mindful Evening Routine Before You Go to Sleep

The Power of Your Subconscious Mind

The subconscious mind is the main driver of our behavior; it is more open and active during sleep. Right before you drift off to sleep is the best time to plant seeds in your subconscious mind to begin the reprogramming process of a positive mindset.

This technique is an extremely powerful method we can implement to make positive changes and manifest our goals.

Replace old limiting beliefs, bad habits, and fears with new positive ones.

Try this mindful evening routine for at least 21 days.

5 Things to Do Before Going to Sleep

1. Leave your smartphone away from your bed or turn it off one hour before you go to sleep.

2. Cultivate mindful thoughts. Each night, go to bed with a positive and uplifting thought, pushing away negative or worrying feelings.

3. Practice gratitude regularly. Expressing thankfulness rewires the brain's molecular structure, maintains healthy gray matter, and contributes to a happier, healthier life.

4. Commit to a positive affirmation about yourself or your life. Identify old, self-limiting beliefs and create a strong, positive affirmation to counter them. For example, if you fear failure, you might say, "I am confident and strong enough to succeed. I have the potential to succeed."

5. Review and repeat your goals every single night.

Incorporate this routine before bed and first thing in the morning. Consistency is key.

My Yoga

I offer myself love. I offer myself peace. I see my beauty. I hear my needs

"NAMASTE... The light and love in me acknowledge and honor the light and love in you."

Yoga

Derived from the Sanskrit word "Yuji," meaning yoke or union, yoga is an ancient system of physical, mental, and spiritual practices that originated in India more than five thousand years ago.

Yoga is a powerful therapeutic tool that addresses our entire nature (physical, mental, and emotional) and empowers us toward personal growth and well-being.

Harvard study researchers found that 12 weeks of regular yoga slowed cellular aging and significantly decreased inflammation in the body.

It can reduce stress and anxiety, increase energy, and improve flexibility and strength in the body.

Yoga, in its physical aspect, is called Asana, which refers to the physical postures (Asanas) that we practice nowadays. However, yoga is not only physical; asana constitutes one branch of the eight limbs of yoga. There are also breathing techniques, meditation, and other rules and principles for our daily life called Yamas and Niyamas.

"Yoga is the journey of the Self, through
the Self, to the Self."

What Are Yamas and Niyamas?

1- Yamas

Yamas are ethical guidelines for living. There are five Yamas:

- ***Ahimsa:*** Practice non-violence in thought, word, and deed; practice self-love.
- ***Satya:*** Tell the truth and be honest; opt for silence if your words may harm others.
- ***Asteya:*** Do not steal, even in non-material ways, such as withholding information or time.
- Brahmacharya: Use your energy wisely, with intention, self-restraint, and moderation.
- ***Aparigraha:*** You are enough and have everything you need already. Don't possess more than you need; you are non-attached and non-greedy.

2- Niyamas

The Niyamas are self-discipline practices. There are five Niyamas:

- ***Saucha:*** cleanliness and purification.
- ***Santosha:*** contentment.
- ***Tapas:*** willpower, hard work, and self-discipline.
- ***Svadhyaya:*** the study of the self.
- ***Ishvara Pranidhana:*** surrender to the divine.

"Be the energy you want to attract."

Sun Salutation A (Surya Namaskar A)

Suryan Namaskar (or sun salutation) is a very beneficial yogic exercise. It is a flow of physical postures practiced together to energize and warm your body. It stretches your muscles gently and prepares your body for more advanced postures. It calms the mind and helps improve concentration.

Regular practice of Surya Namaskar gives strength and vitality to the body.

The best time to practice Sun Salutation is early morning or evening. You must practice it on an empty stomach or at least 2 hours after having a meal.

Be mindful of your body and breath while moving. Link one breath to one movement.

As a beginner, learn to listen to your body and do not overstretch. Repeat the sun salutation three to five times.

> "Calming the mind is yoga. Not just standing on the head."

On days when you don't have time for a long practice, this sequence of poses can quiet your mind while boosting your energy and giving you the stretch and activation you need to have a calm, productive day.

1. To begin, bring yourself to the front edge of your mat and start by standing with your feet together or slightly open. Establish a slow, steady rhythm for your breath and find your center.

2. Inhale, raise your arms over your head, and look up.

3. As you exhale, fold slowly all the way down (modified: you might bend your knees if you cannot touch the floor).

4. Inhale halfway up, look forward, press your hands into your shins or thighs (depending on the flexibility of your hamstrings), and keep your back parallel to the floor and your shoulders away from the ears.

5. Exhale. Place your hands on the floor next to your feet and step back into a plank. Bring your knees to the floor with your hips up, and start by lowering your chest and chin first to the floor while sliding forward.

6. Inhale, lift your chest into cobra position: your palms are placed on the floor next to your chest, your shoulders are rolling back and pulling away from your ears, and your elbows are pointing back and forth. Press the tops of your feet and thighs onto the floor while lifting your kneecaps. Breathe

7. Exhale and push yourself into the Downward-Facing Dog position (inverted V): Your feet are hip-distance apart, your hands are shoulder-distance apart, you are pressing the floor away from you, and your arms

are straight. Lift your hips while pressing your legs back, trying to reach your heels down towards the floor (modified: you can bend your knees to lengthen your spine). Breathe; stay here for 3 to 5 breaths.

8. At the end of the exhalation, walk your feet toward the front of the mat. Inhale, and lift your torso halfway parallel to the floor.
9. Exhale and fold forward all the way down.
10. Inhale as you lift up all the way into standing while maintaining the length of your spine.
11. Exhale and bring your hands together in front of your heart.

Sun Salutation A (Surya Namaskar A)

My Meditation

I am calm.

"As we become aware of our thoughts, we begin to realize how much our own unhappiness is caused by the stories we tell ourselves."

Most of our internal life happens in our heads, where there is so much noise.

There is a time when we have to learn to tune in to our hearts and listen.

The Benefits of Meditation

- During meditation:
- Your stress hormone levels decrease.
- Your blood pressure decreases.
- Your brain waves go up.
- You release dopamine (the feel-good hormone).
- Your grey matter increases.

- Your digestive system relaxes.
- Inflammation in your body is reduced.

> "You live most of your life inside your head. Make sure it is a nice place to be."

Night Time Meditation

- Set your phone to silent mode and place it out of reach.
- Find a comfortable position in a quiet space, seated or lying down, and gently close your eyes.
- Relax the muscles in your face, neck, and shoulders, and begin to focus on your breath.
- Pay attention to the sensations in your body.
- Perform a full-body scan from your toes to the top of your head. Identify any areas of tension or discomfort. As you focus on these areas, breathe deeply to release any tension.
- Observe the gentle rise and fall of your belly with each breath.
- Allow your breath to be soft and deep. The more deeply you connect with your breath, the more deeply you connect with yourself.
- Let your breath reach every part of your body, including the deeper dimensions of your heart. Notice how it feels.
- If you encounter pain, release and let go completely.
- Center your awareness inward. Find that space inside your heart, and take a slow, deep breath to soften your heart.
- As you inhale, visualize your breath as pure, healing energy nourishing your entire body. As you exhale, imagine toxins, stress, and stagnant emotions leaving your body through your fingers and toes.
- With each inhalation, you become more relaxed.

- With each exhalation, you go deeper.
- Silently repeat to yourself, "I am well, I am safe, I am calm."
- Continue focusing on the rhythm of your breath until you drift off to sleep.

"Quiet the mind and the Soul will speak."

My Mindful Meditation

- Find a quiet and comfortable place to sit on the floor. Ensure your head, neck, and back are straight but not rigid.
- Feel the support of the earth beneath you, allowing yourself to be grounded and held.
- Become mindful of your breath, focusing on the sensation of air moving in and out of your body. Notice your belly expanding and contracting like a balloon, and feel the air as it enters and exits through your nostrils.
- If your mind wanders, gently observe where your thoughts have gone. Avoid ignoring or suppressing them; acknowledge them without judgment and gently return your focus to your breath. Use your breathing as an anchor and remain calm. Be kind to yourself if you find your mind drifting.
- Sit still for a minute or two, concentrating on your breath and surroundings.

"The goal of meditation isn't to control your thoughts. It is to stop them from controlling you."

The Meditation of The Heart

In the meditation below, you will be guided to listen to your heart's messages, clearing away any blocks to reconnect with your true nature and inner voice.

"Learn to think from the heart."

Follow these simple steps to connect with your heart's energy:

1. Begin by sitting comfortably and closing your eyes. Place your right hand over your heart and your left on your belly.

2. Release your thoughts and the outside world for this moment, allowing yourself to be fully present.

3. Direct your attention to your heart center, in the middle of your chest, and be aware of your heart as a space. Feel the rhythm of your heartbeat and notice how your right hand rises and falls with each breath.

4. Breathe gently and allow your breath to flow into your heart. You may choose to visualize a soft, pastel light infusing your heart center, soothing and healing it.

5. As you continue to breathe softly, ask your heart what it needs right now.

6. Spend the next 5 to 10 minutes simply listening. Your heart may begin to release long-held emotions, memories, wishes, fears, and dreams. Receive these without judgment and allow them to flow out.

7. Your breathing might change—you may gasp, sigh, or feel tears. Let

these experiences unfold naturally. If you daydream or drift into sleep, gently bring your focus back to your heart center.

8. Inhale deeply, and as you exhale, release all heavy emotions, such as anger, fear, resentment, guilt, or sadness, from your chest. Visualize them dissipating like clouds in the sky. Then, with a deep inhalation, fill your heart with a sense of peace, pure love, and calm.
9. Repeat silently to yourself, "I allow the love in my heart to heal me."
10. Remain still for a moment, and when you feel ready, gently open your eyes.

"You will always find the answer in your heart where it has been waiting since long before the question."

Getting in touch with your heart center allows you to listen more deeply to your true inner voice and connect to the flow of life.

The heart's message is always right.

You can register on our website to join our online healing studio, where you'll gain access to our extensive library and monthly free group sessions focused on heart connection, breathwork, meditation, and yoga.

Part III - My Healing Space

My Little Corner

I feel. I heal

"What you resist persists."

Like a physical wound, you need to learn how to clean and heal your emotional wound. At the core of healing is self-awareness.

Be aware of your inner world and your pain. Allow yourself to feel it and express it.

Don't resist it. Resisting hurts worse than the pain itself.

Learning to express your feelings will help you become more self-aware, leading to increased mental and physical health.

Writing for just 3 minutes, two days in a row about a negative experience has emotional and physical benefits. Most ancient cultures pointed to a connection between the body, the mind, and the emotions and recognized that each composed a part of the whole.

Our thoughts direct how we feel and our emotions strongly influence and affect our body and health.

"Allow yourself to feel the thing that you are afraid to feel: Feel it and be Free."

It is Safe to Express Your Emotions

Learn to Identify Your Emotions

Are you feeling sad, angry, or anxious?

Take time to be aware of what you are feeling in the present moment and try to separate each emotion. Crying is okay; it is a pain reliever and mood regulator.

Each time you feel down and need to let your emotions out, use "My little corner" to release what is hurting you.

Transform your pain into growth.

"Our emotions are energy in motion. When your emotions are blocked, your energy is stagnant and you are subject to sickness and diseases."

- ***If I am feeling sad***, I allow myself to feel my feelings and write them down.
- ***If I am anxious***, I take some deep breaths in and out and focus on the present moment.
- ***If I am lonely***, I call someone I trust or go out.
- ***If I am stressed***, I make time for self-care.
- ***If I am not confident***, I remind myself of my strengths.

"The pain you feel today is the strength you feel tomorrow. For every challenge encountered, there is an opportunity for growth."

5 Things to Remember When You Are Going Through Tough Times

1. Everything will change. Nothing is permanent.
2. You learn and grow the most through pain, discomfort, and change. We all go through hard times; this is part of life.
3. You will get what you want at the right time; be patient.
4. You are not your thoughts; stop stressing out about them.
5. You always have the power to choose your reaction. External factors and the statements of others have no power to hurt you unless you allow them to.

"At the core of healing is self-awareness."

Heal: Emotional Well-Being and Mental Health Exercises

Choose the exercise you need:

1. If you deny your feelings, → Exercise 1: How am I feeling? Allow yourself to feel your pain.
2. If you feel unsafe/anxious, → Exercise 2: I feel safe.
3. If you are sad and lonely, → Exercise 3: I feel good and grateful.
4. If you only see your imperfections, → Exercise 4: A love letter to myself.
5. If you need comfort and spiritual connection, → Exercise 5: A letter to the divine and my angels.
6. If you need to finish a painful chapter, → Exercise 6: A goodbye letter to someone or a situation that made me suffer.
7. If you lost your heart flame and your motivation, → Exercise 7: I am alive; I reconnect with my heart.
8. If you are disconnected from yourself, → Exercise 8: The moment of truth, reverse the negative habit.
9. If you are a victim, → Exercise 9: Take your power back.
10. If stress is your only companion, → Exercise 10: Dear Stress, "Let's break up" letter.
11. If you live in fear, → Exercise 11: Face your fears.
12. If you need to let go, → Exercise 12: It is time to let go.
13. If you feel angry, → Exercise 13: Release your anger.

14. If you need to set boundaries, → Exercise 14: Learn to say "No" to express your needs.

15. If you are self-critical, → Exercise 15: Meet your inner critic/a self-acceptance letter.

16. If you feel unworthy, → Exercise 16: I am a valuable being.

17. If you are hopeless, → Exercise 17: Letter to my future self.

18. If you are stuck in your stress, → Exercise 18: I smile with all my body and heart (quick stress relief).

19. If you hold yourself back, → Exercise 19: Healing with love.

20. If you are hard on yourself, → Exercise 20: Meet your inner child

It is Time to Learn About Your Emotions

If trauma is the disconnection from ourselves, healing is the reconnection.

The mind often repeats what the heart needs to heal.

We often attempt to escape our pain, pretending it has disappeared, yet it lingers beneath our struggles, fears, and unhappiness. The peace, joy, and freedom we seek lie on the other side of the pain we don't want to feel. Feel that pain, and be free.

Disease serves as a message from our bodies, highlighting the areas where we are not free—where we still suffer and where healing is needed. These are the places that require our love, attention, and care.

Much of the pain we experience in life stems from trapped and suppressed emotions resulting from past traumas and unresolved situations.

Emotions are "energy in motion," and allowing them to flow freely without resistance is essential. When these energies become blocked within us, they remain trapped in our nervous system, disrupt our lives, and manifest as illness.

When we suppress our emotions, we also suppress our needs and, consequently, our true selves. This detachment from ourselves leaves us vulnerable to illness as our bodies express what our voices cannot. Our bodies say "no" when we fail to voice it. It is crucial to recognize that emotions are our friends, not our enemies; they are our allies on our journey toward self-awareness and fulfillment.

In many cases, disease or anxiety is a message from your body that you are not okay, you are detached from yourself, and your body is out of balance.

Emotions are messengers that help us identify our needs. They guide us towards our unmet needs and deepest desires, urging us to pay attention and take action. **They are the mirror of our inner world**. Emotions are not inherently positive or negative; they can be classified as pleasant or unpleasant. If we find ourselves experiencing an unpleasant emotion, it's important to remember that they are not inherently "negative." There's no need for self-judgment or avoidance. Emotions are integral to our development. By embracing and understanding them, we can fulfill our innermost needs and ultimately live more authentically, leading to a healthier and more fulfilling life.

Always remember...

Healing means aligning with your authentic, true self; illness is moving away from that alignment, from your heart's desires and soul call.

Unfortunately, the adaptive response to our early environment often involves some learning mechanisms to suppress our authenticity and needs to gain acceptance and a sense of belonging. This behavior emerges from a deep-seated fear of losing protection and security, which is particularly needed during childhood. As children, we instinctively prioritize attachment to our family and parents. The desire to belong and be accepted is closely intertwined with our need for protection and nurturing. We may suppress our true selves, desires, and authentic needs to conform to the expectations and norms set by our parents and society as a whole. This adaptive response is a survival mechanism that ensures we receive the care and support necessary for physical and emotional well-being.

However, as we grow, it becomes important to recognize and address these adaptive behaviors. We must learn to connect again to this authentic self and create a balance between maintaining our true self-expression and seeking a connection with the external world. This process of self-discovery and self-acceptance is crucial for our overall well-being and personal growth, as it allows us to reclaim our truth while maintaining healthy connections with others.

The loss of authenticity is a significant cause of illness, physical and mental distress. The remedy lies in returning to ourselves, reconnecting with our hearts, and learning to accept, respect, and love our precious and valuable selves.

The Root Causes of Anxiety

"Recognizing the source of your anxiety is the first step toward reducing its impact on your life. This awareness allows you to soften your perception of anxiety and approach it with understanding rather than resistance."

Anxiety often arises from unresolved emotional issues such as past traumas. It can be triggered at any time by one or more factors and/or incidents that might awaken an old fear and a deep insecurity.

It is happening more nowadays for many reasons, mainly because of the speed of change we face in the world in all aspects. Most of us don't feel safe anymore. We are losing control over things we used to control. **We are challenged to make quick changes, release the old, and surrender to the unknown**. The big challenge is to know how to make a healthy transition; if there is resistance, there will be anxiety, but if we are well equipped with the right tools to learn how to accept and navigate change, the process becomes easier.

It is time to start unlearning what we used to learn. **We can feel safe not by controlling but by surrendering to the heart's intelligence and trusting the flow of life**. The source of any discomfort is resistance: resistance to change, to letting go, to moving on, to forgiving, to forgetting, and to accepting.

Anxiety hides underneath mainly one or more of the following:

1- Fear of the Future/Unsafety:

Anxiety can stem from a deep-seated fear of the future or an insecurity about certain aspects of life where you feel unsafe (sense of danger). It's essential to identify what you're trying to escape, what you're attempting to anticipate, and where these fears originate. Understanding these underlying fears is an important step in addressing anxiety. When anxiety arises, it's crucial to recognize that it is often related to past experiences that your body once experienced. Remind yourself that those events are over, and you're safe now. Your body retains the memory of the trauma. When we **release the emotional pain of the past**, the body releases the memory of the trauma, and the mind heals. Through the heart, we can heal, stop resisting the pain, release it, and move on.

2- Loss of Control:

Modern life is marked by rapid changes and an increasing sense of losing control over various aspects of our lives. The urge to control often masks a fear of failure, a lack of confidence, or a sense of unworthiness. In some cases, it's driven by a fear of losing something or someone, often tied to past traumatic experiences. The fear of death or abandonment is one of the most common sources of insecurity. What are you trying to push away from you by exerting control? Why is control so important to you? The constant need to control may give us the illusion of safety, but true security comes from surrendering to the change process without resistance. It's important to recognize that when you try to control a situation, it's often because you're anticipating a danger that isn't real. Remember, the mind tends to imagine worst-case scenarios—what we refer to as unjustified fears. Embracing the present moment, releasing the past, and accepting change are vital in managing anxiety. We are part of a vast, intelligent universe where some things are beyond our control, and learning to surrender and trust the process is key.

3- Dissociation From Self and Suppressed Needs:

Another common source of anxiety is a disconnection from your authentic self—your truth, your heart's desires, and the inner voice of your soul. Many of us feel lonely, unloved, or unaccepted; we spend our lives trying to conform to societal expectations, losing ourselves in the process. Society often teaches us to seek external validation and conform to societal norms, which can lead to detachment from our true selves. But who decided these rules were valid? Who set these standards? In this battle to fit in, we often lose touch with who we truly are.

External vs. Internal Validation: How much of your anxiety stems from trying to keep up with an endless race you never signed up for but was imposed on you? Learn to say no.

How much of your anxiety stems from feeling inadequate? Understand that you are a valuable human being and that you are enough. You have been created by the same energy and from the same source that created the oceans, the sky, the trees, and the mountains. How can you be less than that?

So anxiety can be connected to denying your needs and true self or not fully accepting certain aspects of oneself. This disconnection often occurs because you might be suffering or carrying deep-seated pain. In response to this pain, you may unconsciously suppress your needs, escaping from them by seeking solace in the external world and living through others rather than embracing your own identity. Learn to express and release your pain, allowing yourself to stop fleeing from it. When you embrace living according to your own values, you liberate yourself from the need for external validation.

4- Playing an Unauthentic Role:

Most of our tensions and frustrations come from compulsive needs to play the role of someone we are not. Sometimes, anxiety peaks when you find yourself playing a role that no longer resonates with you when you find that the road you traveled took you away from your truth. It's essential to ask what role I can't play anymore and which part of me needs attention. The response here is to learn to say no when you can no longer play a role that doesn't align with your authentic self and to say yes to your heart.

> "You often feel tired because you've done
> too little of what sparks a light in you and
> too much of who you are not."

5- Disconnection From The Heart's Energy:

How to Heal: Healing occurs through reconnecting with the heart. Embrace the power of your heart's energy to restore balance and well-being."

Healing and Alignment

Healing is aligning with one's authentic self and needs. Illness, whether physical or mental, is moving away from that alignment. Returning to self-acceptance, forgiveness, and authenticity is the path to recovery.

1. **Accept and Acknowledge:** Acknowledging and releasing your pain is the first step of healing. Recognize that every experience has contributed to your growth, no matter how challenging or painful. Accept your past, wounds, and imperfections as integral parts of your story. By acknowledging them, you can move forward with a sense of self-liberation.

2. **The Wisdom of the Heart:** In a world that often prioritizes the mind, it's time to trust the wisdom of the heart. Your heart holds the key to faith and love, which can guide you through challenging times. The two main ingredients for the "surfing life" recipe are learning to trust the process and stop resisting change. *Anxiety is a coping mechanism; it is the language of fear. Love is the language of healing.* Love is the most powerful force for healing and transformation. It is the language of acceptance and self-compassion. By loving and forgiving yourself, you initiate the healing process. Love helps you mend the disconnection between your external and internal worlds and brings harmony to your inner self. Love, in all its forms, is the bridge that facilitates this journey of healing and self-reconnection. Learn to trust your heart's wisdom; it will guide you in the right direction. Healing begins at the end of resistance and the beginning of surrender.

3. **Embracing Authenticity and Freedom:** It's time to stop running from yourself and start living the life of your dreams. You will express what is hurting you, what you need, and who you are. Do more of what makes you happy, open your heart to give and receive love, and dare to follow your soul's path. This journey is about self-discovery, self-love, and liberation from the judgments of others. You will start living from your heart's abundance, not your fears' lowest energies. You deserve love, respect, and happiness. You deserve to be free.

Know Your Triggers

•□When does anxiety arise? Describe the situation and environment around you.

•□What thoughts or feelings preceded your anxiety spike?

•□What are you experiencing physically—what sensations arise in your body when anxiety occurs?

If you're ready to embark on a transformative journey to overcome anxiety, release your emotional pain, and reconnect with your authentic self, we invite you to enroll in our online courses.

Subscribe to our newsletter to join our anxiety workshops and become a member of our online healing studio. Stay updated and gain access to valuable resources for your journey toward healing and well-being.

https://healbythewellnessbox.com

My Inner Healing Exercises

Exercise 1- How Am I Feeling?

A- How Am I Feeling Right Now?

Identify your set of emotions and feelings, name them, write them in this circle (or in the lines below), and describe them. Write down whatever applies to your case in the lines below. You can use the hints in the grid below. If you don't have any negative feelings, please proceed to section E of this exercise.

Sad	Angry	Stressed
Anxious	Lonely	Unsafe
Guilty	Ashamed	Hurt
Afraid	Disgust	Worried

Allow Yourself to Feel It.

B- Why Am I Feeling That Way? What is My Emotion or Feeling Trying to Tell Me? Is There Anything I Can Change to Feel Better?

____

____

____

____

C- Three Things I Can Do to Change The Way I Feel

1. Breathwork: deep breathing
2. Move your body: go for a walk, do yoga, exercise...
3. Write down three things/people/situations you are grateful for in your life.

____

____

____

D- Take What You Need

Write down whatever applies to your case in the lines below. You can use the hints in the grid below.

Love	Rest	Hope
Inner-Peace	Care	Strength
Safety	Patience	Faith

____

____

E- How Am I Feeling Now?

Write down whatever applies to your case in the lines below. You can use the hints in the grid below.

Grateful	Calm	Peaceful
Positive	Safe	Happy
Grounded	Strong	Hopeful

____

____

Exercise 2- Anti-Anxiety Practice

Shift From Your Mind to Your Heart

When anxiety arises, it's crucial to recognize that it is often related to past experiences that your body once experienced. Remind yourself that those events are over, and you're safe now. Your body retains the memory of the trauma. When we release the emotional pain, the body releases the memory of the trauma, and the mind heals.

Anxiety can stem from a fear of the future or a feeling of insecurity (sense of danger) about certain aspects of life; you feel unsafe. It's essential to understand that if you are trying to control any situation, it is because you are anticipating a danger that is not real, and you have unjustified fears. Understanding these underlying fears is a crucial step in addressing anxiety. Remember that the mind tends to create the worst-case scenarios. Shift your attention to your heart and remind yourself that you are safe even if your mind is playing tricks on you. Take a moment to look around and notice that there is no immediate threat—right now, you are safe.

Write down three moments and/or places that make you feel safe:

____

____

____

Your Safe Haven

Now, you will visualize and create your personal safe haven—a place where you can feel safe and relaxed. This could be a familiar location, a favorite spot, or even an entirely imaginary place that brings you peace and happiness.

1. First, ensure you are comfortable and in a quiet setting. Close your eyes and take a few deep breaths in and out, extending the exhalation longer than the inhalation. Focus your attention on your heart center, imagining this space expanding with each breath in and releasing any tension with each breath out. With every breath, allow yourself to relax more deeply and let go completely. Soften your facial muscles, relax your whole body, and let your mind and heart become at ease.

2. Now, picture yourself on a small path leading to a beautiful place that evokes calmness, safety, and serenity. Envision your surroundings as if you are truly there. Notice every detail—the colors, the sounds, the smells. Allow yourself to feel completely relaxed, happy, and peaceful. This is your safe haven.

3. Continue to explore and savor these beautiful sensations until you feel a soothing energy infusing your entire being. Imagine this energy as a soft, golden healing light that infuses your body from the inside out, making you feel protected and peaceful. You may silently repeat the affirmation, "I am safe, I am protected."

4. When it's time to conclude your visualization, bring your focus back to your breathing for a few moments. When you feel ready, gently open your eyes.

Carry these feelings with you throughout the day or before bedtime, and visit your safe place whenever needed. Remember, you are always protected.

Tips to address anxiety:

1. Calming your nervous system through movement (yoga, physical activity, dance, walking in nature...) and breathing techniques can be very helpful.

2. Remind yourself that you are safe at this very moment. Use the 333 rule to ease anxiety and calm your mind: Identify and name three objects you see and three sounds you hear, then move three parts of your body.

3. You can wash your face with cold water, drink some water, and swap out caffeine.

Connecting with Your Deeper Self: When you experience anxiety, it signals a lack of safety and a disconnection from your needs and true self. Acknowledge your feelings honestly and openly, without denial. Later, work on addressing and releasing your fears and pain through therapy. Reassure yourself with the understanding that, just as anxiety has surfaced in your life, it can also dissipate over time when properly addressed.

Remember that you are more than your mind, body, or story; you are an eternal soul. You exist with or without the stories that have shaped you. There's a deeper layer of yourself, your true essence, which remains constant regardless of circumstances. Building a connection with this profound self allows you to understand the lessons you are meant to learn from the stories unfolding in your life. It is your soul's pathway to growth, inner peace, and self-realization.

Please refer to the root causes of anxiety section.

Exercise 3- I Feel Good and Grateful

Each time you feel sad, upset, or lonely, try this exercise to overcome your negative emotions.

Bring your attention to your heart center and close your eyes each time you are trying to find an answer to the following questions:

1- Recall a very pleasant experience from a time in your life when you were truly happy.

____

____

2- Write down three things you love to do and a beautiful place where you love to be.

____

____

____

3- Remember one positive situation/event from the past for which you are grateful in your life.

____

____

4- Write down the name of someone who brings joy and love to your heart. Imagine them smiling at you.

____

5- Write down three things/people that you are thankful for in your life.

____

____

____

6- Notice any positive changes or sensations you are experiencing in your body, such as a feeling of comfort or softness.

____

____

7- When you finish, read your answers out loud.

Exercise 4- A Love Letter to Myself

Write down three strengths you possess:

___

___

___

Write down two tough times you've made it through:

___

___

Write down two big achievements:

___

___

Write down three personal qualities or skills that you have:

___

___

___

Be Proud of Yourself.

Acknowledge the difficulties you have endured in your life and the fear you have faced.

Acknowledge your strengths and that you are born to be real, not perfect:

No one is perfect, and failure is part of life.

I am proud of myself.

Even if I am not perfect, I accept my flaws because I am a beautiful human being created with love.

My flaws and strengths make me who I am.

Together, they form the essence of my character, making me unique and authentic. Embracing both my flaws and strengths allows me to have a deeper appreciation of my journey.

Signature

....

Now, write a love letter to yourself. Be your own support system and encourage yourself to be fully alive and to live the life of your dreams.

Dear ____________,

____

____

____

____

____

Always remember to be gentle with yourself.

Exercise 5- A Letter to The Divine and My Angels

You Are Not Alone. You Are Loved Unconditionally

Write down three blessings you are grateful for:

____

____

____

Write down clearly your dearest wishes, and immerse yourself in the belief that they have already come true. Allow yourself to fully experience the joy and satisfaction of achieving your desires. Visualize yourself living out the scenarios you yearn for as if they are happening right now. Embrace the sensations of joy and gratitude that arise within you, letting them fill every part of your being. Doing so elevates your vibration to a higher frequency of love and appreciation, aligning yourself with fulfilling your dreams.

____

____

____

What heartfelt message do you wish to convey to your angels? What would you express if you had the opportunity to communicate directly with them? Take a moment to consider the words and sentiments you would share, reflecting on the guidance and support you seek from them.

Exercise 6- A Goodbye Letter to A Person or A Situation That Made Me Suffer

Dear ______________,

What made you suffer?

Write what you feel...

____

____

____

____

____

I need to bid you goodbye because it is time to let go of what is not meant for me and what no longer serves me so that I can grow and become a better person.

Thank you for being part of my journey and teaching me lessons. But now I deserve to be happy and to move on.

Tomorrow is a better day.

Signature ______________

Exercise 7- I Am Alive, I Reconnect With My Heart

What makes you happy? What makes you feel alive?

____

____

What is your heart's deepest desire? What is your dream?

____

____

Do you remember when you were completely aligned with your heart? When?

____

____

What is your gift?

____

____

What drives you?

____

____

When are you most inspired, motivated, and charged up? How can you do more of that starting today?

____

____

How do you feel after reconnecting with your heart?

____

____

Remember "There is a voice that doesn't use words, Listen". Your heart holds all the answers the mind refuses to see.

"The purpose of your life is to find your gift. Find it in your heart."

Exercise 8- The Moment of Truth, Reverse The Negative Habit

Answer "Yes" or "No" for each of the following questions:

1. Do you feel disconnected from yourself or others? _____
2. Are you disconnected from your body? _____
3. Are you disconnected from your emotions? _____
4. Are you disconnected from your own needs? _____
5. Do you tend to the needs of others before your own? _____
6. Are you an anxious person? _____
7. Is your self-esteem based on how you look? _____
8. Do you love yourself? _____
9. Do you have difficulty saying NO to others? _____
10. Does the opinion of others matter to you more than your own opinion? _____
11. Do you pressure yourself to be nice and please others rather than express your feelings?□_____□

If the majority of your answers are YES, then the truth is that you are disconnected from your true self. This is a wake-up call to start working on reversing the YES answers and reconnecting to yourself again before your body starts expressing energy imbalance through physical or mental discomfort.

Review your answers and spend a few moments reflecting on how you would feel if any of your answers were reversed. Write down what steps you need to take to start changing your situation and connecting with yourself, your needs, and your heart. As you reverse the answers, write down your feelings and focus on the beautiful sense of freedom this brings.

For example, if you often feel anxious, imagine how you would feel if that experience were no longer part of your life.

____

____

Put your strategy to make the change you need into action; start with baby steps:

____

____

You Are Important and You Matter. Believe in Yourself.

"We repeat what we don't repair."

Exercise 9- Stop Being a Victim and Take Your Power Back

Define the situation or the person who makes you feel like a victim.

Dear [Name or Title],

I have allowed you to control my thoughts, my emotions, and my life and to pollute my being with your insecurities and toxicity.

I felt ______________________________, and I still feel ______________________________. (Release your emotions here.)

You made me feel insecure and lowered my self-esteem. I lost trust in myself, and I allowed you to damage the sacred relationship between me and myself.

I don't deserve this. I am learning to honor myself and put an end to any toxic relationship or situation that threatens to ruin my life.

For_____ years, I gave you so much power over my life, but now, it's over. I refuse to be a victim. I choose to reclaim my power and release everything that no longer serves me.

I deserve a new chance to be happy and to trust myself and my life again. I am open to receiving what I truly deserve: love, peace, and respect.

From now on, I declare you out of my life and out of my system. I choose to love and value myself, regardless of anyone or anything else.

From this moment, I am free and strong.

*Date:*___________

*Signature:*___________

Exercise 10- Dear Stress, "Let's Break Up" Letter

Dear Stress,

I cannot handle the fear, insecurity, and anxiety you bring into my life anymore.

I've allowed you to control my thoughts, my emotions, and my whole life for far too long, and it is time to put an end to this suffocating relationship and learn to honor my body and mind.

From now on:

I will slow down, listen to what my body and spirit need, and rest and relax. Yes, that's right. I no longer feel like I have to "keep up" with impossible standards and unfinished jobs.

I will prioritize my mental and emotional well-being by choosing myself and my peace of mind first.

I will protect my energy by saying no when needed.

I will no longer allow you to interfere in my relationships; I will focus on healthy connections and leave behind toxic ones.

I will continually seek to let go of you, moment by moment, choice by choice, so that I may fill myself with peace and love instead.

I've come to realize that I am a better person without you, and I deserve to be healthy and happy.

*Signature*____________

Write down your major stress and the steps you can take to reduce/eliminate them:

____

____

Write down your minor, indirect stress and the steps you can take to reduce/eliminate it:

____

____

Write down three things you will do:

1- To take care of your body and protect it from stress

____

____

2- To prioritize your mental health and peace of mind

____

____

3- To protect your energy and create boundaries

Exercise 11- Face Your Fears

Ten steps to sit and deal with your fears:

1. Face your fear, sit with it, and don't ignore it: define what fear(s) you are dealing with.
2. Breathe deeply, lengthening your exhale until it is longer than your inhale; practice deep breathing for a few rounds.
3. Now, acknowledge that fear is irrational most of the time, and our minds tend to create worst-case scenarios that almost never come true.
4. Remind yourself of a pleasant experience, a positive thought, or something or someone that means a lot to you. Shift your attention from a negative scenario to a positive one. Remember that we are always protected; a life force within us vibrates power and love.
5. Remind yourself of three things/situations/people that you are grateful for in your life. Focus on your blessings.
6. Break the stagnant energy of fear by moving your body: do yoga, exercise, etc.
7. Write about your fears: write down all that you feel.
8. Talk to a trusted person about your fear or find a therapist to help you overcome it.

9. At a later stage, when you are relaxed and not anxious, try to figure out the worst that could possibly happen from the situation that causes this fear and imagine yourself handling it; you'll see that you have the inner strength to deal with it and that you can always overcome it. It is all in your mind.

10. Ultimately, do the following exercise: let your fear speak to you.

Remember that fear hides in the shadows of our minds to stay in control. When we bring this fear into the light of day, much of the weight and burden it carries behind the scenes dissolves.

A Letter to Yourself From Your Fear

Dear (Insert your name here_____)

I am your fear of_____, and I want you to know that,

I am sorry if I let you feel imprisoned most of the time and kept you from pursuing the life you want. But my purpose in your life was to protect you from _____(this was my way to convince you that I am useful to you).

However, I know that you, too, have a purpose in life and a dream to fulfill, and I want to help you achieve it and live it freely.

To get rid of me, you need first to face me and understand where I am coming from, maybe your childhood or some other insecurities. It is okay; all people face challenges in life and deal with different types of fears. Challenges help people grow; the key is to focus on progress, not perfection.

One piece of advice to help you break my cycle is to be more alive and in action instead of being lost in your mind all the time. Decide to make the change you need and do it.

Live life fiercely, and you will see that my shadows will gradually disappear.

I wish for you to reach a point where your choices reflect only your dreams, not your fears.

You have the power to choose... Choose life.

Sincerely,

Your fear.

Once the fear is brought to light, it turns from this threatening shadow monster under the bed, into a helpless caring creature in need of some understanding.

Be gentle with it, and understand that fear is in your life for a reason.

Find it, face it, and work on it to be free.

Exercise 12- It's Time to Let Go

What would change for me if I could let go of all the fears I have? What kind of life would I live? How would my life be different, and what could I accomplish if I let go of everything not serving me?

Feel your heart expand as you realize the possibility of living freely and lightly, unburdened by the weight that once held you down. Let the sense of liberation fill you, as if every breath makes you lighter, more at peace, and open to life's endless potential without constraints.

____

____

____

I am willing to let go of the following:

____

____

____

____

____

____

What do I need to do to start the process of letting go? (Change my daily routine, ask for professional help, etc.).

Exercise 13- Release Your Anger

What made me angry?

____

____

____

Write your anger down:

____

____

____

Take a moment to notice that it is not only about the other person or the external circumstances but also about you. What was triggered in you?

____

____

____

What feeling is hidden behind my anger? Am I scared, hurt, depleted, lonely, or sad? Where is it all coming from?

____

____

____

What do I need to calm down? Remember to send love to the part of you that is in pain. Breathe and let go.

____

____

____

Exercise 14- Learn to Say No, to Express Your Needs

When you say "No" to others or things you don't want to do, you say "Yes" to yourself.

It is not selfish to do so; it is a duty towards yourself and others. When you force yourself to say yes to things you don't like to do, you are infusing this act with negative energy that is subconsciously directed to others and yourself.

To whom or what do you need to say "No"?

Complete the sentences below, read each one out loud, and notice how it makes you feel.

Say, "No, I can't."

____

____

Say, "I need my time alone." Say, "I need my space."

____

____

Say, "I need a break."

____

____

Say, “I am afraid you have to wait because now I can’t.”

Say, “I want this.”

Say, “I don’t want this.”

Say, “This doesn’t suit me.”

Say, “I need this.”

Say, “I don’t need this.”

Say, "I deserve this."

Say, "I don't deserve this."

Say, "This is not my problem."

Say, "I didn't agree to this."

Say, "This doesn't belong to me; it belongs to you."

Say, "This is your choice, not mine."

Exercise 15- Meet Your Inner Critic

It's time to observe your inner narrative and notice how it controls you. If self-attack, self-judgment, self-doubt, and comparison dominate your inner dialogue, it's time to change it. This indicates a lack of self-love. Remember, this inner voice might echo the voices of your parents or teachers from your childhood. You internalized it because, as a child, you believed what you were told. Now, it's time to use your own voice—the one you use with friends—filled with kindness, compassion, forgiveness, love, and care.

You are not what your inner critic tells you. Your story does not define you. You are YOU, a being of love and light. Be gentle with yourself and work towards making constructive changes, free from judgment and low self-esteem. When love and acceptance are present, judgment fades away. Self-love means honoring and respecting yourself, both in your brightest moments and through your darkest struggles. It's embracing the full spectrum of who you are—your strengths, flaws, and everything in between—with compassion and love.

When you recognize your inner critic, remember two things:

1. This part of you needs your gentle love and care the most.

2. Would you speak to your friends in the same harsh way you speak to yourself? You must learn to care for your feelings as you do for your friends and loved ones.

Learn to accept yourself with all your flaws and strengths.

To My Dear inner critic,

I accept my flaws and imperfections,

they make me who I am.

Thanks for sharing your opinion

but my mistakes help me grow.

I will look for what I can

learn from this experience.

Best wishes

Signature:

____

Repeat those affirmations:

I am compassionate and kind to myself and others.

I accept and love all parts of myself, which make me who I am.

I am a real person, not a perfect one, and this is what makes me human and unique.

You can continue this exercise by doing exercise 4, "A Love Letter to Myself," which will help you remember your strengths, skills, and qualities.

Exercise 16- I Am a Valuable Being

Read the text below every time you feel unworthy.

I feel valuable and worthy even if others do not approve of or value me. I determine my own value and self-worth by being who I am at my core. In essence, I am a creature of love. I don't need to prove anything to anyone to be valued or loved; I am already valuable from the moment I exist. I was born a human being, not a human doing. Everything I decide to do later will emanate from my free will and desire to live happily, not from my need to please others.

I accept who I am with every part of myself, including my flaws, fears, and behaviors. This is who I am, and I am at peace with that. With love and acceptance, I can learn to make the change I need and have the power and choice to do it. My value comes from within and from the love I was created with. I came to Earth for a purpose, which is to listen to my heart, and this is my biggest value. (Read it out loud)

Many people find the above hard to believe, but with time and practice, we can learn to trust and feel our value.

Write down your biggest value:

Exercise 17- A Letter to My Future Self

Write a letter to your future self. Set goals for who you want to become and outline the changes you want to make and the things you want to keep. Reflect on the most important values and lessons you want always to remember. Consider who you want to be and where you want to be. Visualize this future version of yourself living happily and fulfilling your dreams.

Believe in this vision with love and respect, and commit to working towards making it a reality.

Use the present tense when writing about your future, as if you are living it right now.

____

____

____

____

____

What important message does your future self have for you?

Exercise 18- I Smile With All My Body and Heart

Have you ever experienced smiling with every cell in your body? Let us do it.

Close your eyes and start smiling with your full face. Smile with your eyes, your lips, your cheeks, your ears...

Your brain, head, neck, throat, and shoulders are smiling.

Your heart is smiling, and your lungs, stomach, kidneys, liver, intestines, and genitals are all smiling.

Your veins are smiling.

Your thighs, bones, knees, legs, feet, and toes are smiling, as are your arms, hands, and fingers.

Your whole body is smiling.

Your breath is smiling; your soul is smiling. Your whole being is smiling.

Write down how you feel now. What are the sensations of your body and heart?

____

____

Do this exercise each time you feel stressed; even if you need to fake the first smile, do it; your whole body will respond gradually.

Exercise 19- Healing With Love

Tune into your heart and ask yourself:

- What would it feel like if I loved and accepted myself as I am without judgment?
- What would my life be like?
- What would be different? What actions would I take?

____

____

____

After writing your answers, you will notice that you are the one standing in your own way. Everything lies in your own hands. You and only you can decide your life, yet you are scared to believe in your own power. It is easier to focus on your flaws and failures rather than reclaiming your whole life.

Value yourself enough to dare to live; you deserve to be happy. The choice is yours, and your life is yours—it is only yours to live.

Exercise 20- Meet Your Inner Child

1. If your inner child is standing before you, looking at you right now, what will you see in her/his eyes? Is there any pain or fear? What does she/he need to tell you? What does she/he need the most?

____

____

2. What will you do to make her/him feel better? Maybe you can hug her/him and tell her/him, I am here now for you to take care of you.

____

____

3. Remember what she/he used to love, what made her/him happy.

____

____

4. If your inner child is looking at you right now, will she/he look up to you, or is she/he still expecting another version of you—the one she/he used to dream of? What is this version?

____

____

5. What advice does your inner child have for you?

____

____

6. How can you both be friends again? Can you do one thing now to make your inner child happy? Maybe you can have more fun or offer your inner child a gift.

____

____

Healing Techniques

To learn more about healing techniques and programs, visit www.healbythewe llnessbox.com or call +961 76 539 111.

- ***Biodecoding®*** (Ecole de Biodecodage Christian Fleche-France) is a pioneering technique for decoding any symptom (physical and emotional) and resolving its underlying bio-emotional cause through a signature methodology. It is a complementary approach to conventional and alternative treatments and has the potential to unlock and speed up the healing process. It is an innovative approach to illness and emotional healing.
- ***NLP (Neuro-Linguistic Programming):*** Understand your thinking, behavioral patterns, and emotional state, and work on changing your old perception and limiting beliefs. It is a pseudoscientific approach to communication, personal development, and psychotherapy created by Richard Bandler and John Grinder in California, United States, in the 1970s. NLP's creators claim there is a connection between neurological processes (neuro-), language (linguistic), and behavioral patterns learned through experience (programming) and that these can be changed to achieve specific goals in life.
- ***Yoga Therapy with Chinese Meridians***: Yoga goes beyond the physical aspect, exploring our edges where resistance arises and allowing our

deeper journey to unfold. Detecting the energy imbalances with Chinese medicine techniques and unblocking them to heal and release physical and emotional pain.

Want to dive deeper into the exercises in this book? The accompanying workbook is available as an ebook at www.healbythewellnessbox.com/heal-workbook, offering unlimited printable templates to help you integrate these practices into your daily life.

My Feelings, My Emotions

My Feelings, My Emotions

I Allow Myself to Release Them All

Let The Words Flow Freely

My Energy

**"We heal by releasing not by suppress-
ing."**

Everything in the universe is made of energy and has a vibrational frequency. Energy is constantly moving throughout our physical bodies and electromagnetic fields, vibrating at varying speeds.

A person's health is impacted by the frequency at which their body vibrates. If our body's energy is vibrating at a low frequency, we will be subject to all kinds of diseases. Many habits can lower your vibration: fear, negative mind, unhealthy diet, stress, less sleep, inactive body, alcohol, living in the past, holding onto anger...

Emotional pain can also block the flow of energy in your body. Emotions are stored in your body like memories in your brain. If emotional pain is not released from our body, our energy will be blocked, causing physical tension and illness.

Healing is all about restoring the balance and flow of energy in our body.

> "You have the power to choose. Choose Love."

How Can We Release the Energy Block and Restore Balance?

One of the best ways to do this is to circulate more energy or *prana* throughout the body.

Prana is our life force, our body's natural intelligence. When it flows properly, our body's innate healing power is activated.

The goal in times of challenge is to raise our vibration so our bodies and minds can rest and digest all that is happening around us.

Many ways can restore balance and the flow of energy in our body.

> "If you want to find the secrets of the universe, think in terms of energy, frequency, and vibration."

5 Practices to Raise Your Vibration

1. ***Breathwork***: Any pranayama or breathing technique can balance and restore your energy vibration, but heart-focused breathing is the most beneficial. It is a powerful way to quickly awaken your heart center, raise your vibration, increase your radiance, and access your heart intelligence. Breathing with awareness into the heart center naturally draws more light into it and increases vibration. (Refer to exercise number 7 in Part II, *The Heart-Focused Breathing*, and to the meditation of the heart section of Chapter 18—*My Meditation*.)

2. ***Yoga:*** Regular yoga practice helps you channel your energy and control your focus to be more present. Motion generally unleashes emotion, and movement is essential to unblock our stagnant energy. Whenever it feels difficult to connect with your emotions, move your body: run, do yoga, etc.

3. ***Eating healthy raw food:*** Eat the rainbow (refer to *the five elements of life* section in chapter 9) and avoid sugar, junk, and processed food.

4. ***Positive mind:*** practice gratitude, appreciation, openness, acceptance, kindness, compassion, peace, trust, joy, forgiveness, connection, surrender, happiness, inspiration, creativity, contentment, and harmony. They can all raise your vibration.

5. ***Love:*** Love is the highest frequency at which we can vibrate. When we live in the vibration of love, our energy resonates at a high frequency. Being "love vibrational" is choosing love over hatred, anger, and judgment.

"Whatever you ask for in your prayer, believe that you have received it and be grateful for it."

What I Think, I Feel... What I Feel, I Vibrate... What I Vibrate, I Attract

What thoughts and feelings are you nourishing?

What we nourish becomes the foundation of our energetic field, building the vibration we emit to the world, which will be reflected back to us.

If you feed your energy with the frequency of gratitude and love, you will attract more of this positive energy.

If you cultivate fear, anger, and hatred, you will vibrate at the same frequency as those feelings and attract more of them into your life.

Register on our website to join our online healing studio and unlock access to our extensive sound healing library, offering a wide range of tools and resources to support your journey toward inner peace and well-being.
www.healbythewellnessbox.com

Be The Energy You Want to Attract.

"To heal is to touch with love that which
you previously touched with fear."

Your beliefs become your thoughts.

Your thoughts become your words

Your words become your actions

Your actions become your habits

Your habits become your reality

What we think, we become

Exercise: The Healing Energy

Energy follows mental awareness: When you focus on a zone in your body that needs healing, you draw energy into this part of your body to open it.

Learn how to release your stagnant energy. Set a pure intention to clear your energy.

Healing energy exercise:

1. Wash your hands with soap and water to cleanse and prepare. Dry them thoroughly, then rub your palms together for several seconds to generate warmth. Feel the soothing heat in your hands.

2. Set a healing intention in your mind, allowing it to resonate deeply in your heart.

3. Lie down on your back, close your eyes, and take slow, deep breaths in and out. Begin by gently scanning your body with your hands, attuning yourself to tense or stagnant areas.

4. Place your hands on the area where you feel blocked or stuck. Connect with this space in your body, acknowledging the sensation without judgment. Simply be present with what is, breathing deeply.

5. Visualize the energy within you flowing like a soft, gentle breeze, clearing away the tension. Feel the warmth of your hands enveloping this part

of your body, and direct your attention there, sending love and healing energy.

6. Let this process unfold naturally, without effort or resistance. Surrender fully to the moment, allowing your body to heal in its own time.

7. Remain connected for a few minutes, allowing the energy to work its magic. Feel the release as you let go.

By Being With What It Is We Liberate Energy.

My Mandalas

I De-Stress My Mind

Mandalas have been used in many therapeutic environments to help people unearth feelings that need to be expressed and to clear and relax the mind.

Coloring mandalas is a great meditation technique that can relieve stress and anxiety.

Each time you need to de-stress, open your wellness journal and choose your mandala.

Turn on your favorite soothing music and let the colors flow.

You can download and print the workbook, complete with beautiful mandalas, directly from our website.

Your journey doesn't end here—it evolves.

Continue nurturing your body, mind, and heart with the workbook.

Download the ebook at www.healbythewellnessbox.com/heal-workbook to enjoy unlimited templates, ensuring your healing practices can grow with you.

Join Our Support Group

"Healing is not a journey you need to take alone. Surround yourself with people who understand, support, and inspire you."

We're excited to invite you to our community—a safe space where you can connect with like-minded individuals, share your journey, and support one another in the process of healing and self-growth.

Why Join?

- Access to exclusive resources and live wellness events.
- Connect with individuals who share similar experiences.
- Receive expert tips and guidance from wellness practitioners.
- Share your progress, ask questions, and find encouragement.

How to Join Our Community

1- Visit the Website:

Alternatively, you can visit:

www.healbythewellnessbox.com/community

2- Follow Us on Social Media:

Stay updated on events and announcements by following our official pages:

Instagram: @HealByTheWellnessBox and @TheWellnessBox.lb

Facebook: TheWellnessBox

4- Need Help?

For any issues, please email us at info@healbythewellnessbox.com or call our support line: +961 76 539 111.

We Can't Wait to Welcome You!

Joining the community is a small step that can make a big difference in your healing journey. Let's grow, heal, and thrive—together.

About Lana Fayad

Lana is a certified psycho-bio-therapist in Biodecoding and an NLP practitioner.

As the visionary behind the Wellness Box concept and the accomplished author of Heal: The Wellness Journal, Lana's expertise resonates deeply with those seeking to embark on their personal journey of healing and self-discovery.

Her self-development journey began 15 years ago with profound self-exploration and healing. Over the years, she immersed herself in many energy healing practices, including Reiki and Quantum Touch. She delved into Ayurveda yoga therapy, using the art of Ayurvedic healing nutrition.

Lana's passion thrives in unveiling the authentic self and aligning with the soul's purpose. Through her practical experiences and personal challenges, she has learned to navigate life with a wide range of healing techniques, which she now shares in her book—a culmination of years of study and practices in wellness and self-development. She believes that self-compassion is the key to growth and healing. Lana shows we can build physical strength and mental resilience by nurturing the heart and emotional well-being. Her book offers readers an accessible path to educational healing, filled with practices and a new program designed to foster daily growth and fulfillment.

Like everyone, we sometimes lose sight of what matters, get stuck in our thoughts and emotions, and get caught up in our day-to-day problems. With a healthier mind, heart, and body, the Wellness Journal Heal will guide you to live with more purpose and alignment with your heart.

Subscribe to our newsletter and join our online healing studio to access exclusive workshops, programs, and monthly master classes focused on the latest in healing and wellness. Stay updated with valuable resources designed to support your growth, healing, and well-being.

www.healbythewellnessbox.com

Made in the USA
Columbia, SC
22 September 2025

70019482R00127